IN SEARCH OF GREAT BRITAIN AND NORTHERN EUROPE

IN SEARCH

OF

GREAT BRITAIN

AND

NORTHERN EUROPE

PUBLISHED BY THE READER'S DIGEST ASSOCIATION LIMITED

LONDON   NEW YORK   MONTREAL   SYDNEY   CAPE TOWN

Originally published in partwork form,
Des Pays et des Hommes,
by Librairie Larousse, Paris

A Reader's Digest selection

IN SEARCH OF GREAT BRITAIN AND NORTHERN EUROPE

First English Edition Copyright © 1992
The Reader's Digest Association Limited, Berkeley Square House,
Berkeley Square, London W1X 6AB

Copyright © 1992
Reader's Digest Association Far East Limited
Philippines Copyright 1992
Reader's Digest Association Far East Limited

Originally published in French as a partwork,
Des Pays et des Hommes
Copyright © 1984
Librairie Larousse

Translated and edited by Toucan Books Limited, London
Translated and adapted by Andrew Kerr-Jarrett

ISBN 0 276 42049 7

Printed by Printer Industria Gráfica S.A., Barcelona

Contents

COVER PICTURES

Top: The Langdale Pikes from Chapel Stile in the
Lake District National Park, Cumbria.

Bottom: A Lapplander near Kautokeino
in northern Norway.

The Nation States of the Northern Seas

The call of the sea, of conquest and of trade, links the nations of north-western Europe's Atlantic fringe. From the Viking marauders of the 8th century onwards, to Elizabethan England's buccaneering sea dogs, to the traders and missionaries who laid the foundations of the British Empire, right down to the 20th century's North Sea oil workers, the peoples of these sea-girt lands have braved the oceans and the perils of unknown continents to seek their fortunes or spread their faiths.

For the Norsemen of ancient Scandinavia, it was probably the pressure of numbers on their mostly barren native soils that drove them overseas. They are chiefly remembered for the terror they inspired in western Europe's coastal and riverside dwellers. But their dragon-prowed longboats carried settlers to Iceland and Greenland and almost certainly reached Newfoundland and modern Canada. To the south the Vikings established themselves in Scotland, Ireland and England, raided Moorish Seville in AD 844, sacked Pisa in Italy, and proceeded as far as Sicily. In the east, meanwhile, their kinsmen from Sweden made themselves masters of the waterways of eastern Europe as far south as the Black Sea.

The year 1066 is the most famous date in British history. William the Conqueror and his knights – themselves the descendants of Norse settlers in France – soon brought England under their control and before long their offspring had spread Norman influence into the Lowlands of Scotland, across Wales and into Ireland. The mingling of peoples in the British Isles – Celts, Angles, Saxons, Vikings, Normans – produced a talented brew. Freedom-loving and resourceful, the British more or less invented modern democracy and industry. By the late 18th century a now unified Britain was the richest nation on Earth; by Queen Victoria's Diamond Jubilee in 1897, it ruled a huge proportion of the Earth – the British Empire encompassed a quarter of the world's population.

The 20th century has been marked by astonishing changes. Britain, battered by two World Wars and industrial decline, has lost its Empire and is left torn between allegiances across the Atlantic to America and across the Channel and North Sea to Europe. Ireland has established its own independent state (not including the six counties of Northern Ireland) and in Wales and Scotland nationalist sentiments are on the rise. Scandinavia has seen equally remarkable transformations. Countries that 100 years ago were little more than impoverished backwaters now boast some of the highest living standards in the world. Finland, which for most of the century has had to tread a delicate path to preserve its freedom from the former Soviet Union, is world famous for its architects and designers. Sweden, Norway and Denmark are widely regarded as models of social democracy. Iceland prospers, thanks in part to its exploitation of geothermal resources. Even Greenland's ice-bound inhabitants, though still nominally part of Denmark, have broken free from the European Community and are seeking to go it alone in a rapidly changing world.

Great Britain

Despite centuries of political union, the three countries that make up the island of Great Britain retain their own special characters and traditions. England – the largest, richest and most heavily populated of the three – has long been the dominant partner, but the two Celtic nations of Scotland and Wales have added their touch of intuitive flair to the British character. Together the people of Great Britain, sheltered behind their island's natural sea defences, have proved freedom-loving, inventive and resilient.

Lakes, mountains, open
moorlands, pine forests and
sheep are the basic
constituents of much of the
scenery of central and North
Wales.

This solidly built farmhouse
tucked away in a valley in
West Wales seems the very
picture of rural peace. The
large front porch is a common
feature, providing protection
against the elements in a
region where the annual
rainfall is generally high.

Previous page:
For grand occasions, whether
Ascot, Trooping the Colour or
a large family wedding, the
British still know how to put
on a good show. There is a
certain timeless and
endearing elegance about the
British woman's hats and
white kid gloves and the
perfect cut of the man's
morning coat.

The Road to the West

Strange things happen in Wales during the first week of August. Early each morning, a group of men strangely clad in flowing druidic robes gathers in one of the towns of the principality – a different town every year, alternating between North and the South. Some of the men carry trumpets and horns; one bears an impressive ceremonial sword. They form a procession and then, accompanied by hundreds of followers and onlookers, they wind their way to a small circle of stones, usually set on a hilltop outside the town. Another day's proceedings at the Royal National Eisteddfod of Wales are about to begin.

Wales is famous for its mines. But the principality as a whole is one huge mine, and a remarkably undiscovered one at that. Most people know about Welsh rugby, singing and coal, but the resources of Wales go much deeper than that. Its landscape is impressive enough: the mountains of the North, the lush agricultural valleys of the south-west and Mid Wales, the rocky headlands of the Pembrokeshire coast. But perhaps more remarkable even than these is the wealth of its culture. Wales can boast the oldest living language in mainland Britain, and in literature, especially poetry, an unbroken lineage stretching back to the 6th century AD. All of this is remarkable testimony to the staying power of an ancient Celtic people, pushed back into Wales's rugged fastnesses by successive invasions of Angles, Saxons and Normans, yet still clinging to many of their age-old patterns of life.

Of all Welsh institutions the National Eisteddfod is among the most characteristic. Although it emerged in its present form only in the late 18th century and became an annual event in the mid-19th century, the eisteddfod is rooted in a tradition that goes back to the times of the bards who sang at the courts of the Welsh princes and princelings of old. Admittedly, the druidic trappings of the National Eisteddfod are rather less authentic – they were mostly concocted by a Glamorgan stonemason called Iolo Morganwg, who came up with the idea of a druidic Gorsedd (Session) of Bards, and held the first ceremony in 1792, in London's Primrose Hill. None the less, they add an attractive touch of typically Welsh wizardry to the proceedings.

In essence, the Eisteddfod is a kind of Welsh Olympics of the arts. Early in the year chapels and working men's institutes throughout Wales organise small, local eisteddfodau – competitions in poetry, singing, drama, the arts and crafts. The winners of these go on to take part in larger, regional eisteddfodau, and the winners of these can compete in the National Eisteddfod.

This being Wales, the singing competitions are eagerly followed. To be a 'National Winner' confers great prestige and can lead to a promising career; the

This small boy and his grandfather both have the unmistakable dark eyes of the Celt. Behind them rises their fine old black-and-white house, the decorative timbers marking it out as a dwelling of some distinction. Timber-framed buildings are typical of the lush agricultural valleys that line the Mid Wales border with England.

Welsh opera singers Sir Geraint Evans and Gwyneth Jones both started as National Winners. But perhaps the key event for most Welsh people is the competition for the best *awdl* or ode.

The architect Sir Clough Williams-Ellis chose a remote peninsula in north-west Wales as the site for his Italianate fantasy village, Portmeirion. His buildings there include a complete campanile, a castle and a lighthouse, but others are no more than façades.

Wales's mountain heartland

North-west Wales is a region of mountain, wild moorland, lake and forest. Rising dramatically to the east of the treacherous, swift-running waters of the Menai Strait, the four great peaks of the Snowdonia heartland – Foel Fras, Snowdon itself (at 3560 feet the highest mountain in Great Britain south of the Scottish border), Glyder Fawr and Carnedd Llewelyn – form a kind of prow facing into the Irish Sea. To the west protrude the rolling, fertile acres of the island of Anglesey, once covered with forests where the authentic druids of Celtic Britain performed their rites before they were vanquished by the Romans in AD 61. To the east extend more mountains which merge into the northern ranges of Wales's high backbone, the Cambrian

As in so many streets in Welsh and English towns, the basic structure of the houses may be the same, but their owners have made each one distinct. Doors are painted in different colours and are sometimes decorated with bronze knockers, shaped like imp's or dragon's heads or dolphins. Windows are carved out in different shapes and sizes, and peeping from inside are some of the householders' prized possessions – here, a Staffordshire china dog downstairs and upstairs a porcelain pig.

Mountains. Their sides are roamed by Welsh Mountain sheep and dotted with isolated granite farmhouses and tiny villages. Around the mountains' edges, coastal strips provide perching places for the north-west's chief towns: Porthmadog, the castle town of Caernarfon, and the cathedral and university city of Bangor.

This wild corner of Wales can truly claim to be a heartland of Welsh culture. It was to the mountains of the north-west that the independent Welsh princes retreated time after time to regain their strength as they fought the remorseless encroachments of the Norman kings of England. Today, the north-west is one of the great bastions of the Welsh language. Two-thirds of its people have Welsh as their mother tongue, a higher proportion than in any other part of the principality.

The people here are a hardy, resilient race. And a talented race, too, who have probably produced more than their fair share of famous sons. The 'Welsh Wizard', David Lloyd George, Liberal Prime Minister from 1916 to 1922 and the man generally regarded as Britain's saviour in the First World War, grew up near Criccieth, west of Porthmadog. Lawrence of Arabia was born at Tremadog, just outside Porthmadog. And the architect Sir Clough Williams-Ellis came from an ancient local family. His chief memorial is the extraordinary Italianate fantasy village of Portmeirion, which he built on a wooded bluff east of Porthmadog.

Today, the little village of Aberffraw on Anglesey's south-west coast is a sleepy place set at the head of an attractive cove. Once, however, it was a seat of princes and capital of Gwynedd, for long the most powerful of the independent Welsh princedoms. Gwynedd's golden age was in the late 12th and 13th century, the age of the Llywelyns. It was Llywelyn the Great who, more than anyone, succeeded in holding back the Norman conquest of Wales. After the death of Llywelyn's grandson, the Welsh war for independence finally collapsed in 1283. Edward I consolidated his victory by building a great chain of castles around the country – Conwy, Beaumaris, Caernarfon, Hope, Ruthin, Flint, Rhuddlan, Aberystwyth and Harlech – and in 1301 had his young son, the future Edward II, proclaimed Prince of Wales, a title borne ever since by the British monarch's eldest son.

Harlech, perched dramatically on a crag over what was once a tidal creek, is probably the most impressive of the Edwardian castles. From 1404 to 1409, it housed the court of Owain Glyndwr, leader of Wales's last major bid for independence. The rebellion was effectively quelled and Glyndwr escaped. Nearly 80 years after Glyndwr's defeat, his kinsman Henry Tudor came to the English throne as Henry VII, and in 1536, under Henry VIII, the First Act of Union was passed, integrating Wales with England.

Welsh women are proud of their national costume. Even today, on special occasions, many of them wear the distinctive wide skirt, white or coloured shawl, and tall black beaver hat perched on top of a lacy bonnet.

A marked individualism is one of the notable characteristics of the Welsh, seen perhaps in their choice of the leek as well as the more obviously decorative daffodil as national emblems. Each year on March 1 the people of the principality celebrate St David's Day. They commemorate their patron saint – a South Welsh bishop of the 6th century AD – by wearing either a daffodil or a small leek in their lapels.

Farming, slate and tourism

With its wild beauty and rich history, modern north-west Wales relies heavily on tourism. Indeed, Wales as a whole depends very substantially on the tourist industry. It was estimated in 1991 that tourism employed some 9 per cent – around 95,000 people – of the total Welsh work force and brought £1.5 billion into the principality each year. In the north-west the dependence is all the greater for the decline of traditional local industries.

A century ago slate was king, and it was through slate that coastal towns such as Porthmadog grew. Slate, which has been quarried in Snowdonia since Roman times, was exported through Porthmadog to the four corners of the huge British Empire, and the industry employed thousands of local men. Nowadays, just a few

quarries remain operational, such as those near Blaenau Ffestiniog. The chief memorials to past glories are the numerous narrow-gauge railways that ply between the mountains and the coast. Where once they transported cargoes of slate, they now carry families of tourists.

The other traditional mainstay of the local economy is farming. Except in the fertile, lower-lying areas such as Anglesey and, farther east, towards the English border, the Vale of Clwyd, sheep farming predominates. In recent years, the traditional small family holdings have found it difficult to survive. Increasing numbers of families – who may have farmed the same land for generations – have been forced to sell up.

In the circumstances, tourism seems the obvious saviour. But even in the heart of the north-west, where tourism has been more restrained, there are problems; for example, the former farmhouses bought as holiday

homes by English people. The new owners certainly preserve the houses, often attractive old granite buildings, but rarely live in them for more than a few weeks in the year, thereby making little contribution to the local economy, and adding to the problem of depopulation. Even worse, they help to push up house prices in the region, making it harder for young families to buy their first homes. A certain local resentment against the outsiders is inevitable.

West Wales, the long arm jutting out south of Cardigan Bay, offers an altogether gentler landscape than the north-west. The southern reaches of the Cambrian Mountains form the backbone of this region, and are flanked by broad coastal lands which reach the sea in high, dramatic cliffs, craggy headlands and

beautiful, often sandy coves. On the northern side of the mountains, the River Teifi (on which some local fishermen still go out after salmon in round coracles that have scarcely changed in design since the Iron Age) has carved out a wide and fertile valley leading into Cardigan Bay. To the south, the Towy flows into the Bristol Channel. It is a region much loved by walkers, sailors and surfers.

Near the region's westernmost tip, the huge fjord-like inlet of Milford Haven forms one of the finest natural harbours in the world. In the 1790s, its potential was spotted by, among others, a group of perhaps some 50 Quakers emigrating from Nantucket. Whaling was once an important industry here; nowadays, however, it is vast modern oil-tankers, not whalers, that you will see

The seaside resort of Aberystwyth houses Wales's first university college, opened in 1872, as well as the National Library of Wales, which has one of Europe's finest collections of materials relating to Wales and other Celtic countries. A cable railway climbs to the top of Constitution Hill, where there are fine views along the huge sweep of Cardigan Bay.

steaming through the narrow, 1½-mile strait at the mouth of the inlet. Milford Haven's deep waters and 70 miles of sheltered coastline make it ideal for these bulky sea monsters. The town that shares its name has become one of Europe's leading petroleum ports. Long rows of oil-storage tanks rise on the skyline, and the flares of oil refineries cast a lurid glow into the night sky.

Running roughly west to east from Roch, not far from the coastline of St Bride's Bay, to Kidwell, Llanstephan and Langharne, a curious language boundary called the *Landsker* slices through the old counties of Pembroke and Carmarthen. North of the *Landsker*, Welsh is the mother tongue of most locally born people; to the south it is English, and has been for nearly ten centuries. The reason for the division probably dates from the time of the Danish raids up Milford Haven. The dividing line between the Welsh and the English is roughly at the

Two smartly turbaned ladies enjoy tea and scones in a tea shop on the seafront at Aberystwyth. Since the Second World War the growing popularity of holidays abroad has meant a decline for traditional British resorts. The waters of the Mediterranean may be warmer than those of Cardigan Bay, but places such as Aberystwyth still have plenty to offer: magnificent scenery nearby, the narrow-gauge Vale of Rheidol Railway, and the remains of a 13th-century castle, built by Edward I of England and captured in 1403 by the Welsh nationalist leader Owain Glyndwr.

limit of Danish penetration. The Normans eventually built castles along the line, and the southern part was settled in English style with big estates, a pattern which survived as long as it did in England. The name generally given to Pembrokeshire, 'Little England beyond Wales', applies, therefore, to the southern part.

Before the Normans, Pembrokeshire was home to Wales's patron saint. The place that bears his name, St David's, is tucked away in a fold in the hills in the Welsh-speaking part of Pembrokeshire. It can claim to be the smallest city in Britain – by virtue of its 12th-century cathedral, but it is in reality no more than a largish village.

Standing on a bluff above the Towy Estuary, and dominated by its castle, Carmarthen is a picture of prosperity. It is the chief market town for the rich dairy-farming area of the Towy Valley, and its modern county offices bear witness to its importance as the administrative centre for the new county of Dyfed, created when the old counties of Carmarthenshire, Pembroke and Cardigan were merged in 1974.

Wednesdays are particularly busy. Wednesday is one of the three days of the week when Carmarthen holds cattle sales and also one of the two days when the covered market is in operation. Housewives, many of whom have come in from the surrounding country for a

Llanybydder in the valley of the River Teifi in south-west Wales is famous for its horse fair. Once a month horses and ponies are brought here from all over the region and paraded round the The Mart under the expert eye of the local buyers and dealers.

Two young farmers watch the action at a local Welsh livestock market. The small farmers of the Welsh hills need a keen commercial sense, for theirs is a modest living which is further threatened by the possible loss of a number of European Community subsidies.

A farmer displays a prize bull at an agricultural show.

'The leg of mutton of Wales beats the leg of mutton of any other country,' was the enthusiastic comment of the 19th-century traveller George Borrow. The small

Welsh Mountain sheep is distinguished by a long body and brownish face and legs. It is hardy and can survive on the hills and mountains throughout the year.

day's shopping, load up in supermarkets, meet friends in the town's tea shops and pay visits to their favourite dress shops. Farmers take a break from the sales to down a few pints in one of the many pubs and discuss the weather, EC milk quotas and the general state of business. In the covered market, stalls groan under a profusion of vegetables (many of them grown in Pembrokeshire), tender legs of Welsh Mountain lamb and, above all, arrays of local cheeses, including huge truckles of Caerphilly, Llanboidy and Pencarreg.

But Carmarthen's prosperity does not rule out a touch of radicalism. In 1966 its electors made history when

The Welsh are a nation of singers: male-voice choirs and mixed choral societies, many of which reach professional standards, are a feature of many Welsh communities. And Welsh people still enjoy a cymanfa ganu, *a singing assembly, where they spend a day or an evening singing hymns under the baton of a visiting conductor. Here, two young men playing a guitar and a concertina are entertaining customers in a pub with some traditional folk songs.*

they returned the first Welsh Nationalist (Plaid Cymru) member to Parliament in a by-election.

The countryside and coastline south-west of Carmarthen inspired some of the finest work of the poet Dylan Thomas, who lived for many years in Laugharne (pronounced 'Larn') on the Taf and Twyi Estuaries. The town celebrates his memory with a performance every three years of his poetic drama, *Under Milk Wood*. And you can still take a drink at his favourite Brown's Hotel.

In northern Dyfed the landscape takes on a wilder air. The mountains rise higher and come down closer to the sea. The waters of Cardigan Bay glint more grey than blue. Lying in the centre of the huge sweep of the bay is the resort and university town of Aberystwyth.

Welsh people are intensely proud of Aberystwyth's University College, and rightly so, for they had to fight hard to get it. Until the 19th century, Wales had no university. Aberystwyth is home to another key institution of Welsh culture – the National Library of Wales, founded in 1907. The library includes among its treasures the earliest complete text of the masterpiece of medieval Welsh literature, the *Mabinogion*. This is a splendid collection of tales, some set against the background of the court of King Arthur, others

concerning the mythical Welsh prince Pryderi, son of Pwyll, 'lord over the seven cantrefs of Dyfed', as well as Math, son of Mathonwy, lord of Gwynedd, who 'might not live save while his feet were in the fold of a maiden's lap'. They are full of magic, knightly deeds and a shrewd folk wisdom.

King coal

From the world of Pryderi, son of Pwyll, it is a far cry to the world of the 'Valleys', the series of narrow river valleys that gouge sharply into the uplands north of Cardiff, Newport and Swansea. Two hundred years ago, this was a wild and lovely region. From the open moorlands above, streams and waterfalls tumbled down the forested valley sides. Sheep grazed the open ground. The only sign that an industrial revolution was taking place was a narrow ribbon of iron foundries along the top end of the valleys. By the mid-19th century, the scene was rather different. Line upon line of small, tightly packed terraced houses now rose up the valley sides. Pit-head workings rose starkly into the air, grinding periodically as they brought up loads of coal or miners returning to the surface at the end of a shift. Beside them rose black slag heaps. Dank canals, railway tracks and sidings lined the valley floors. The South Wales coalfield – which until the First World War exported all over the world – had been born. Henceforth the names Rhondda, Ebbw Vale and Merthyr Vale would be synonymous with coal.

Sixty years ago, and the scene was different again. Still the bleak terraced houses, the dank canals and the slag heaps. But the pit-head workings were no longer so active, nor the railway lines at the bottoms of the valleys so busy. The Great Depression which lasted from 1929 to the mid-1930s had South Wales in its grip. By August 1932, 245,000 people (out of a population of only 2.5 million) were out of work in Wales as a whole, and the brunt of the unemployment fell on South Wales – on the Valleys and the associated steel areas in the coastal strip to their south. The Valleys never properly recovered from the Depression. In 1945 the output of the South Wales coalfield had been 20 million tons. By 1970 it was down to 13 million tons, and by 1990 it was 3.4 million tons.

For all their miserable back-to-back housing, poor wages and conditions, the Valleys produced a uniquely rich and varied culture. Tightly packed into their narrow ravines, the people of the Valleys to this day show a remarkable solidarity. In hard times they stick together, those with jobs helping out those without. Their ways were affectionately chronicled by the writer Richard Llewellyn in his novel *How Green Was My Valley*, published just after the Depression in 1939.

Like all true Welshmen, the people of the Valleys love to sing, and have produced some of the finest of the great Welsh male-voice choirs, including the Treorchy Male Choir. These choirs have their roots in the Methodist and nonconformist revivals that swept

This peaceful rural pub proudly displays the dragon of Cymru, or Wales. The Red Dragon was officially recognised as the Welsh badge in 1801, and in 1959 the Welsh flag was proclaimed by royal command to be the Red Dragon on a green and white background.

Until the beginning of the 20th century folk dances, which evolved from pre-Christian rituals, were a traditional feature of local fairs and festivals in rural England and Wales. Dancers would clash their sticks, stamp their clogs and often mime events from old folk tales. Recently there has been a revival of folk dancing, particularly the 'morris' dancing associated with ancient spring festivities, and dancers in full costume frequently perform at week-ends outside pubs and at village fêtes.

the Law Courts and the National Museum of Wales.

Cardiff is also home to the great Welsh national rugby stadium, Cardiff Arms Park. The Welsh are rugby mad, and Cardiff Arms Park is one of their holiest places. Rugby internationals at the Park are particularly fine events, where supporters can indulge two great Welsh passions – rugby and singing.

Although the Valleys have continued to decline, the rest of South Wales – traditionally dominated by the steel industry – has experienced a remarkable renaissance in recent decades. Huge amounts of public money have been ploughed into the region to good effect.

The trailblazer in the process was the Lower Swansea Valley Project which, starting in the early 1960s, transformed the area around Swansea from a moonscape of scarred tips and derelict factories into a modern commercial centre, with new factories, schools, houses and sports and leisure centres. By the early 1990s Wales was able to face the future with a certain amount of confidence. Unemployment (8.4 per cent in 1991) was still higher than the average for the United Kingdom as a whole, but it was lower than that of other areas formerly dominated by heavy industry.

Striking east along the M4 from Cardiff and Newport, you reach the old castle and market town of Chepstow. From here, following the beautiful, thickly wooded Wye Valley north to Monmouth, you enter yet another, very different Wales, the Wales of the borders, or 'Marches'. Until recent times, the old county of Monmouth was very much disputed territory. The controversy was finally resolved in 1974, when Monmouthshire, minus a small strip on the border with Mid Glamorgan, became the new, Welsh county of Gwent.

Monmouthshire is a gentle land of rolling hills and woods. But head west and you are back in mountain territory, where the Usk Valley cleaves its way between the Black Mountains and the Brecon Beacons. Striking north again takes you into the heart of the county of Powys. In the fertile eastern parts of Powys, English is spoken, while in the Cambrian uplands of the west most people speak Welsh.

A further lap north takes you to the beautiful Vale of Llangollen in the upper Dee Valley. Llangollen itself is an attractive and busy market town set on the banks of the Dee. Its moment of glory comes in July each year when choirs and splendidly attired folk dancers and singers congregate here from all over the world. They have come to take part in the Llangollen International Music Eisteddfod (not to be confused with the National Eisteddfod), which was started as an annual event just after the Second World War, with the specific intention of helping to heal the wounds of war. For a week the town echoes to the voices of the choirs and to the sound of dancers performing on the bridge over the Dee and in the streets. The Llangollen Eisteddfod has been supremely successful in its role of furthering understanding between nations and it thus forms a perfect complement to the National event. Where the National takes Welsh people back to the roots of their culture, Llangollen opens the arms of Welsh culture wide to the outside world.

Life may be increasingly hard in the Valleys, the traditional coalmining areas of South Wales, but this miner has not lost his smile. The list of the valleys' famous sons is ample testimony to the creative talents of its people: the actor and film star Richard Burton, the novelist Richard Llewelyn, the postwar Labour politician and spellbinding orator Nye Bevan, the opera singer Sir Geraint Evans, and the popular singer Tom Jones.

Wales in the 18th and 19th centuries, leaving as their mark the chapels which, with their strong emphasis on preaching and hymn singing, provided the focal point for most Welsh communities. The chapels may now be comparatively empty, but the choirs – and the old hymns – are still extremely popular.

Wales's young capital

In the space of 200 years Cardiff (*Caerdydd* in Welsh) has grown from being a market town and small port to being, since 1955, the capital of Wales. Cardiff may be young, but it looks every inch the part. Dominating the centre of the city is its magnificent castle. In Cathays Park, the splendidly landscaped Civic Centre is laid out in grand style, rather like a smaller version of the Indian capital, New Delhi. It contains the handsome City Hall,

England's Green and Pleasant Land

'Kent, sir – everybody knows Kent – apples, cherries, hops and women,' comments Charles Dickens's Mr Jingle in *The Pickwick Papers*. One of England's most richly interesting counties has all that, and a lot more. In the first place Kent, thanks to its position as the part of England closest to continental Europe, is particularly rich in history. It was in Kent – probably in the area of modern Deal – that Julius Caesar landed when he made his expedition to Britain in 55 BC. Later, when the Romans started colonising Britain in earnest, they established their first settlements in Kent.

As in so much of south-east England, chalk dominates the Kentish landscape. The chalk sweep of the North Downs emerges from neighbouring Surrey, strikes across the north of the county and then veers south-east before plunging into the English Channel in Dover's famous white cliffs.

The North Downs form the backbone of Kent. South of them spreads the Weald of Kent, a beautiful and fertile land of gently sloping hills and valleys. In the past, crowds of East Enders would come down to Kent in summer to pick the hops – used to flavour the Englishman's traditional pint of bitter. Mechanisation and the contraction of the hop industry in the face of the growing popularity of lager have largely put paid to that attractive custom. The cylindrical oasthouses that dot the countryside are now mostly homes, many owned as weekend retreats by people from London.

Canterbury, on the Downs' northeastern edge, has a time-soaked splendour befitting its dignity as seat of the Primate of All-England and worldwide headquarters of Anglicanism. Large parts of its walls are still intact, and within them narrow streets retain much of their medieval character. Soaring in the centre is the cathedral, where in 1170 Archbishop Thomas Becket was murdered. For centuries after that, Becket's shrine was a great centre of pilgrimage in England, one pilgrimage featuring in Geoffrey Chaucer's 14th-century masterpiece, *The Canterbury Tales*.

From Canterbury the edge of the Downs leads to Dover. While most of Britain's western, Atlantic-facing ports have declined during the 20th century, Dover in the east has gone from strength to strength, a reflection of Britain's growing orientation towards Europe. And west of Dover are the workings of the Channel Tunnel, due to be completed in 1993, realising a centuries-old dream of establishing a permanent link between Britain and mainland Europe.

The sun may be bright but clearly there's a nip in the air as an elderly couple keep on coats and jackets on Brighton's seafront. It was the supposed medicinal qualities of the water at Brighton that first made sea-bathing popular, and led to the resort's 18th-century nickname 'Doctor Brighton'. Among its earliest patients was the Prince Regent, and where he led, many others followed, acquiring a taste for the brisk plunge into the waves.

The reclaimed marshlands of Romney Marsh, along the coast south-west of Dover, present yet another beautiful face of Kent. Pretty villages cluster around ancient churches, while Romney Marsh sheep graze some of the best natural grassland in the world. At Romney Marsh's eastern end, just across the border in Sussex, the old walled town of Rye was once a port, though the sea has long since receded.

Chalk cliffs and the memories of ancient conflicts dominate much of the Sussex coast. At its eastern end the old fishing port of Hastings is famous for the battle in which William the Conqueror defeated the Saxon King Harold in 1066 – in fact, the battle was fought a few miles inland where the town and ruined abbey of Battle now stand.

West again is the great resort of Brighton. Superb white-stuccoed terraces of Regency houses line its seafront, while a few yards inland rise the improbable domes of the Prince Regent's oriental fantasy, the Royal Pavilion, completed in 1822. Every weekend during the summer, crowds of visitors descend on Brighton from London to explore the antiques shops of the narrow Lanes, enjoy a ride on Volk's Electric Railway, stroll along the great wrought-iron Palace Pier, or even take a dip from England's first nudist beach.

Surrey – much of it merging into the southern sprawl of London – is for many people more or less synonymous with commuters. It is the heartland of the businessman living in a comfortable detached house, catching the same train into 'Town' and then returning home each evening at as near the same time as

London's infamous suburban railway network will allow him to.

Surrey is also one of southern England's prettiest counties. Around Dorking in the eastern fringes of the North Downs, rivers have cut through the chalk to form dramatic, beech-covered gorges. To the west the impressive, double-edged escarpment of the Hog's Back – once a haunt of highwaymen – cuts across country from Guildford to the old wool town of Farnham.

West of Surrey, crystal-clear and trout-filled 'chalk streams' weave their way across rich arable farming land in central Hampshire, where chalk uplands emerge once more. At the heart of the county, Winchester is famous for its cathedral, boys' public school and King Alfred the Great, the remarkable 9th-century ruler of the Kingdom of the West Saxons, or Wessex.

Two great ports lie on Hampshire's coastal edge. In the east, Portsmouth has for centuries been Britain's most important naval port. It was from Portsmouth that Nelson set sail to defeat the French and Spanish fleets at the battle of Trafalgar in 1814. More recently, the bulk of the task force sent to recapture the Falkland Islands in 1982 left from Portsmouth. In 1620 the Pilgrim Fathers embarked for North America in Southampton to the west – the start of a transatlantic traffic that was to reach its peak in the first half of the 20th century, the age of the great liners. In their heyday whole rows of these beautiful creatures might be berthed at one time.

Yachting, holidaying and retirement dominate the old royal hunting grounds of the New Forest, south-west of Southampton, and the diamond-shaped bulk of the Isle

Although most English people live in cities, they remain a country race at heart. Many, kept in the cities by their work, look forward to their retirement when they will buy a place in the country, cultivate their garden and enjoy the quiet pleasures of English village life. Many live in the country even while working in the city, commuting long distances each day and enduring the discomforts of none too efficient suburban railway services. The 'home counties' immediately surrounding London are littered with homes such as this – spacious, comfortable and with lovingly tended gardens.

Among the most glorious sights of the English spring are the carpets of golden yellow daffodils that spread along hedgerows and through city parks from April onwards. You can chart the course of spring as they come into flower from Cornwall, along the South Coast, inland and finally up into the colder North.

of Wight sheltering the end of Southampton Water. The New Forest's great oaks were heavily felled in the 16th to 18th centuries to build the ships that provided England's 'wooden walls'. Large tracts of woodland remain, however, intermingled with open heath and grassland cropped by New Forest ponies.

The large cathedral close at Salisbury in south Wiltshire encapsulates much that is typical of the gently

George III's wife Queen Charlotte was one of the early enthusiasts for the products of the great 18th-century porcelain manufacturer Josiah Wedgwood – and he named his Queen's Ware after her. Wedgwood employed the artist and sculptor John Flaxman to create many of the classically inspired designs that are still the hallmark of Wedgwood china.

The English are, of course, famous for their tea. But the full 4 o'clock ritual of tables groaning with tea, toast, sandwiches and cakes has declined in recent decades, as few people can spare the time to prepare it all. Even so, a cup of tea with perhaps a biscuit or two is still an important punctuation mark in most people's afternoon. In the North they have different traditions. People there still enjoy a 'high tea', which includes a hot course, at about 6 o'clock. Northerners also sometimes drink tea with their main midday meal.

paced life of southern England. Rising in its centre is the cathedral itself, capped by a 404-foot spire, the tallest in England. Fringing the close are imposing Georgian houses. Ladies in tweed skirts and gentlemen in tweed jackets guard the tills in the cathedral shop and offer tourists learned accounts of the building's history. It is not hard to imagine yourself in the world of Anthony Trollope's *Barchester* novels with their accounts of 19th-century cathedral-city intrigue.

The broad chalk uplands of the Salisbury Plain to the north are a military area. At their centre the stone circle of Stonehenge, built between 2750 and 1300 BC, has lost some of its romantic feel, as traffic whizzes along the main roads that run on either side.

Avebury in the downlands of north Wiltshire was more important in prehistoric times. It has the largest stone circle in Europe, 1350 feet across. Another 100 pairs of stones lead off in an avenue to the south. The circle was built in about 2500 BC, probably as a religious centre. Modern times re-emerge along the M4 which cuts across northern Wiltshire. Swindon, for example, grew in the 19th century as a railway town. In the last few decades it has grown still faster as a popular place for businesses relocating out of London.

London – city of superlatives

'A man who is tired of London is tired of life,' was the characteristically decisive judgment of the great 18th-century man of letters Dr Johnson. The streets of late 20th-century London may be clogged with traffic, and its public transport system close to breaking point, but it remains one of the most exciting cities in the world.

The largest city in Europe, it is also by far the most cosmopolitan. As well as the immigrant communities mostly congregated in the suburbs, it has large numbers of North American, European and Japanese residents, working perhaps in one of the financial institutions of the City or in the media or for one of the international bodies based in London. Few major capitals dominate the commercial and cultural lives of their nations more than London does, and this helps to explain the huge influx of visitors each year.

London's cultural life has few equals. There are over 40 major theatres and many smaller ones, five full-time symphony orchestras and huge modern arts complexes

Taxis and bright red double-decker buses fight their way along Oxford Street (left). It was a Victorian architect Joseph Hansom who designed the two-wheeled, horse-drawn 'cabs' that were London's first taxis. As for the double-decker buses, they too were originally horse-drawn – they were transport for all, hence their full name omnibus, *from the Latin word meaning 'for all'. Meanwhile, a guardsman and yeoman (right) eye each other up. The bearskinned infantrymen of the Guards, together with their colleagues of the Horse Guards, are soldiers who will see military action if necessary. The job of the Yeomen of the Guard, or 'Beefeaters' (a 17th-century term for well-fed servants), is largely ceremonial. They were formed by Henry VII in 1485 and their uniform has changed little since. They are often confused with the similarly uniformed Yeomen Warders, a body of ex-servicemen whose job is to look after visitors to the Tower of London.*

such as the Barbican Centre in the City and the South Bank complex on the Thames with the Royal Festival Hall and the National Theatre. Major museums include the British Museum (with one of the world's greatest collections of antiquities) and the Victoria and Albert.

Annual events in London range from the royal pomp of Trooping the Colour in June to the West Indian-inspired Notting Hill Carnival in August, from the Chelsea Flower Show in May to the Proms during the summer months.

For many people, London means the West End, with its shops, parks, theatres and great buildings. The traffic circle of Hyde Park Corner is generally regarded as the centre of the West End. From its south-western corner, Knightsbridge heads towards the world's most famous department store, Harrods. The high walls of the Queen's London residence, Buckingham Palace, line the southern edge, while Piccadilly with Green Park to its south sucks traffic away to the east.

Oxford Street, to the north-east, is probably the most famous of London's great shopping streets, lined with department stores such as Selfridges, huge branches of chain stores such as Marks and Spencer and scores of smaller clothes boutiques. Bond Street and Regent Street lead off Oxford Street to the south. Chauffeur-driven Bentleys, Mercedes and Jaguars hover outside the auctioneers Sotheby's and the jewellers Asprey's in Bond Street. In Regent Street children swarm over Hamley's, the world's largest toy shop, while their elders patronise large clothes stores such as Austin Reed and Aquascutum.

At the foot of Regent Street, Piccadilly Circus, with the statue of Eros at its centre, marks the entrance to another part of the West End. Shaftesbury Avenue heading north-east is the heart of theatreland. To its north Soho's grid of narrow streets is lined with restaurants and bars of every kind. To its south lie the streets that comprise London's small Chinatown.

Heading east from Leicester Square at the bottom end of Chinatown takes you to Covent Garden, formerly the capital's fruit and vegetable market. Today the area around the Italianate piazza has many of London's trendiest clothes shops. Tired shoppers sit out in one of the open-air cafés and watch the antics of street entertainers.

The central landmarks of London are more spread out than those of most capital cities. This is because there were originally two cities – the 'square mile' of the City of London, and Westminster, some two miles along the banks of the River Thames to the west. Westminster grew up from the 11th century onwards around a royal palace (its site now occupied by the Victorian Gothic Houses of Parliament) and its Abbey. The twin cities grew in parallel and did not really merge until the 17th

Late in the evening, coming back tired from work or a film or the pub ... what better than to pop into the 'chippie'? Several important decisions await you there. Will it be battered plaice, cod or haddock that you have with your hot mound of chips? And then, do you want salt or vinegar or both on the chips? And do you want the bundle (rarely nowadays wrapped in the traditional newspaper) 'open' for immediate consumption in the car or on the pavement, or 'closed' to take home and eat there? Not that fish and chip shops any longer have a monopoly on the take-away trade. As well as American-style hamburger joints, Chinese and Indian 'take-aways' do thriving business in most English towns and cities.

century: the City, the commercial capital; Westminster, the centre of royal and later political power.

That distinction between the two halves of central London continues to this day. It is Westminster that contains, as well as the shops, theatres and restaurants of the West End, most of the great institutions of political, social and cultural power. Running off Parliament Square to the north is the broad, imperial sweep of Whitehall, lined with the Foreign Office and other great ministries of state. Downing Street, with the Prime Minister's official residence at No. 10, leads off it to the east.

Beyond Westminster lie Chelsea and Kensington – until the 18th century country villages separated from London by meadows. In the 1960s, Chelsea's King's Road was one of the centres of Swinging London, its clothes shops haunted by all young or youngish people

In the background the 'Mother of Parliaments' – in the foreground, members of the large immigrant communities that have settled in most British cities since the Second World War, keeping alive the links with the ex-Empire.

A 'lollipop lady' halts the traffic to let a schoolchild cross the street. Less popular in most motorists' eyes are the traffic wardens who prowl the streets slamming 'tickets', entailing unpleasantly stiff fines, on cars that have stayed too long at meters or are parked at the wrong time on a yellow line at the side of the road.

The pub remains at the heart of English life – and recently the laws that dictate when pubs may or may not be open have been relaxed. But the pub's supremacy is not unchallenged. In city and town centres wine bars are increasingly popular, particularly with young professional people, while for those with an alternative bent there are vegetarian cafés where they can drink strictly caffeine-free coffee substitutes or wholesome glasses of freshly made apple juice.

with a claim to fashion. Sloane Square at the end of the King's Road has given its name to Sloane Rangers, young upper middle-class people living in London, usually identified by loud voices, strings of pearls worn outside turned-up collars by the women, and green wellington boots worn by both sexes when in the country at weekends.

The financial institutions of the City of London play a gigantic role in the life not only of London but also of Britain, and indeed of Europe. Despite recent threats from Frankfurt and the Paris Bourse, the City remains Europe's largest financial centre. A walk through the City is a strange experience. Huge modern office blocks, constantly being built and rebuilt to accommodate more office space, rise from streets with unmistakably

medieval names – Poultry, Cheapside, Cornhill – which still largely follow the medieval layout of the 'Square Mile'. They house banks and financial organisations from all over the world. Sadly, they now all but submerge some of the City's finest architectural landmarks, notably Sir Christopher Wren's St Paul's Cathedral, built between 1675 and 1710 after the Great Fire.

London's rail network was built from the mid-19th century onwards to serve the ever-growing capital. As it grew, the city swallowed communities that were once outlying country towns and villages. Many such as Greenwich and Hampton Court are full of historic interest. Others such as Hampstead, Highgate and Camden have intellectual or artistic associations.

In the years following the Second World War a

Sweet Thames flow softly ...

The Thames used to be the principal means of getting around London. In the time of the 17th-century diarist Samuel Pepys and before, kings, nobles and commoners alike would travel from place to place on magnificently gilded barges or on taxi-style hired craft.

West of London, the Thames flows through attractive rolling countryside. In Berkshire the towers and ramparts of Windsor Castle rise imposingly on the south bank, with the Royal Standard fluttering from the central Round Tower when the Queen is in residence. South of the castle spreads Windsor Great Park, with the town of Ascot on its southern flank. The Royal Ascot race meeting each June is one of the grandest

Beadles (recruited from retired soldiers of the 10th Hussars) are at hand to enforce the rules of the privately owned Burlington Arcade, built in 1819. Inside, the bow windows of the shopfronts display college ties and scarves, hand-made shirts, regimental buttons ... and all the other traditional appurtenances of the English gentleman. From the rear of the arcade it is a short walk to Savile Row, the heart of London's tailoring trade.

massive flood of immigrants from different parts of the former Empire flowed into Britain, and they too have made their mark on London. Walking through Brixton market in south London you might imagine yourself transported to the Caribbean. Stalls offer an enticing array of yams, breadfruits, ackees, mangoes, Jamaican rum and many other West Indian goods. Newsagents and small supermarkets throughout London are now almost exclusively run by immigrants from the Indian sub-continent and their English-born children. The immigrant communities have added an exciting element to London's cosmopolitan mix. There have been problems too, however. In the early 1980s racial tensions in Brixton led on a number of occasions to rioting and ugly confrontations between police and local youths.

events of London's social calendar, attended in force by the Royal Family.

Beyond Windsor and Eton the Thames Valley loops north, then south, then north again. North of Reading the course of the Thames finally reaches Oxford, where by some local quirk the river temporarily becomes known as the Isis. The city 'of dreaming spires' has, in fact, two faces: its academic centre and its industrial outer rim. The centre has all that anyone could ask of one of the world's greatest, and oldest, seats of learning (dating back to the 12th century): magnificent college buildings whose architecture ranges from the medieval glory of Merton College Chapel to the clean modern lines of St Catherine's College built in the 1960s; and the Bodleian, among the world's greatest libraries. Oxford's industrial area is centred on Cowley in the south-east where William Robert Morris, later Viscount Nuffield, started to produce Morris cars in the 1920s.

Chalk hills and new towns

The Chiltern Hills run from just north of Reading through Oxfordshire, Buckinghamshire and Hertfordshire as far as the industrial town of Luton in Bedfordshire. They are a pretty region of chalk uplands, impressive escarpments and wooded valleys. High Wycombe near their southern end, in Buckinghamshire, is an important furniture-making town. Also in Buckinghamshire, north of the Chilterns, is the new town of Milton Keynes, founded in the late 1960s to try to cope with London's overspill.

Hertfordshire has two more new towns – Letchworth and Welwyn (pronounced 'Wellin'), started much earlier, in 1903 and 1919. The man who inspired these projects was the remarkable Sir Ebenezer Howard. His book *Garden Cities of Tomorrow*, first published in 1898 and many times re-issued in the early years of this

In July 1985 tens of thousands attended the massive all-day Live Aid concert in Wembley Stadium, while millions of people around the world watched the proceedings on television. Live Aid was the brainchild of the Irish pop star, Bob Geldof, and was designed to raise money for the victims of famine and civil war in Ethiopia.

The traditional bright red British telephone box (left) – originally designed by the architect Sir Giles Gilbert Scott – has sadly become a thing of the past. Boxes such as these have almost all been replaced with anonymous booths that are, however, less prone to being vandalised.

The British 'bobby' (above), by contrast, remains unmistakable. The police owe their nickname to the politician Sir Robert Peel who was Home Secretary when London's Metropolitan Police Force was set up in 1828.

century, was the first to propose the idea of creating new towns which incorporated rural belts, thus combining the blessings of town and country.

Much of Essex to the east has been swallowed up in the sprawl of London. It has two more new towns at Harlow and Basildon and the Thames-side port of Tilbury. To the east and north, however, the influence of London recedes. The eastern coastline is deeply indented with river estuaries such as those of the Crouch and Blackwater, and has popular resorts such as Southend and Clacton-on-Sea.

West of Clacton, Colchester has important Roman remains. To its north, the River Stour flowing through low hills marks the border with Suffolk. The great landscape painter John Constable was born at East Bergholt, just across the border in Suffolk, in 1776 and regularly painted the countryside around Dedham and Flatford Mill.

'Very flat, Norfolk' runs the famous inconsequential line in Noël Coward's play *Private Lives*. And so it is – as is much of East Anglia. Crossing the countryside west of Norwich in particular, huge level expanses of wheat, barley and beet crops spread out as far as the eye can see. Hedges and walls are few in one of England's most intensively farmed regions, and only the slightest of rises in the ground add an occasional touch of variety to the landscape. And yet the country has its own kind of beauty. Flat lands allow for spectacular skyscapes with dramatic plays of cloud and light.

North from Norwich, the Norfolk coast bends in a semi-circle from King's Lynn in the west. In the days of Norfolk's wool wealth King's Lynn was one of England's busiest ports, trading with the Baltic and Mediterranean. Fine Georgian houses and a 17th-century custom house testify to that prosperity. A few miles to the north lies Sandringham House, the mock-Jacobean mansion built in 1870 for Edward VII when Prince of Wales – traditionally, the Royal Family spend the New Year there.

Wide shingle beaches backed by open areas of marsh

Anarchists, evangelists, animal-rights campaigners, a dwindling band of socialist revolutionaries, people with particular grievances ... all these and more still gather at Speakers' Corner by Marble Arch each Sunday to air their views. Onlookers (usually including vigorous bands of hecklers) move from soap box to soap box, forming large circles around the more amusing or eccentric speakers, leaving others talking to the thin air or a stray dog. The right to free speech at this spot has been guaranteed by law for centuries.

East Anglia and the shires of Middle England

Norwich, rising from a loop in the River Wensum in Norfolk, was England's second largest city from the Middle Ages to the Industrial Revolution. The sheep grazing East Anglia's flat or gently rolling lands provided the wool that fed the pre-industrial looms of England's most important weaving centre.

Norwich is now well down in the league of England's larger cities, and the surrounding farming lands are better known for their wheat than their wool, but it remains a prosperous and an attractive place. Radiating from the great Norman castle at its centre is a warren of streets lined with Tudor, Stuart and Georgian buildings – among them the cobbled Elm Hill where in the Tudor Stranger's Club immigrant weavers from all over Europe used to meet.

Among the elderly the stately pleasures of bowls are popular. As joints grow stiffer and limbs less agile, they can still enjoy the skills of this surprisingly challenging game. And they have distinguished precedents. Tradition has it that the great Elizabethan sailor Sir Francis Drake was playing bowls at Plymouth in the West Country when news came that the Spanish Armada had been sighted.

There are few things the English love better than old things, be they antiques, ancient traditions or, as here, veteran bicycles. Veteran cars are another great love. Each year on the first Sunday in November Hyde Park Corner whirrs to the sound of Rolls-Royces, Lancias and the like for the start of the London to Brighton Veteran Car Run.

and heath line the Suffolk coast south of Great Yarmouth. In between Lowestoft and Ipswich are attractive towns such as Woodbridge, Aldeburgh and Southwold. Aldeburgh was the home of the composer Benjamin Britten and the classical singer Peter Pears, and in 1948 they founded its Music Festival held each June. It seems a smiling region now ... and yet life has traditionally been hard along this coast. Summers are hot, but in winter bitter winds sweep in off the North Sea from the flat lands of northern Europe and Russia. And there has been a constant battle against erosion. Dunwich north of Aldeburgh was Norman Suffolk's most important town, lying at the mouth of the River Blythe. Then in January 1326, in the course of a single night, a storm shifted millions of tons of sand and shingle across the harbour mouth, diverting the Blythe northwards. After that the North Sea ate steadily away at the shallow cliffs along the coast, which collapsed taking whole streets and houses with them. By 1677 the sea had reached Dunwich's market place; by the 18th century most of the town had gone. Around 1920 All Saints' Church tumbled over the edge leaving a single gravestone and a local legend that the peal of its drowned bells could sometimes be heard at night presaging a coming storm.

Inland, low, rolling hills spread across the southern part of Suffolk. Towns along their edges like Lavenham, Sudbury and Bury St Edmunds grew rich on wool. Sudbury was also the birthplace of the great 18th-century portrait and landscape painter Thomas Gainsborough. On the borders of Cambridgeshire is Newmarket, where talk in the pubs is all of horses. The town is the British headquarters of the 'sport of kings', housing the British Jockey Club. Early each morning trainers and jockeys put their horses through their paces across Newmarket Heath.

Trinity Great Court and King's College Chapel (famous also for its choir) are among the architectural glories of the university city of Cambridge, whose first

The Queen presents a trophy to horse-owner, Prince Ahmed Bin Khalid, at Ascot, Britain's grandest race meeting. Royal Ascot is held in the third week in June each year, when London and the motorways leading towards Berkshire buzz with unwonted numbers of hired limousines whisking their occupants to the glories of the Royal Enclosure. For the Royal Family such occasions are more than simply social duties – the Queen and the Queen Mother, in particular, are well-known fans of horse-racing, each owning important racing stables.

college, Peterhouse, was founded in 1281. Behind the colleges green lawns spread down to the River Cam. While the older university of Oxford has traditionally been known for the humanities, Cambridge has nurtured many great scientists, notably the discoverer of the laws of gravity Sir Isaac Newton in the 17th century and in the early 20th century the discoverer of the atomic nucleus Lord Rutherford. Today the university's scientific expertise is exploited in the local computer and high technology industries.

Spreading across north Cambridgeshire and into west Norfolk and south Lincolnshire are the Fens. This is the East Anglian landscape at its flattest and most eerie. The Fens are the product of extensive draining and dyking, mostly in the 17th century.

In the north, the Fens spread around the flat bottom edge of the Wash, which makes a box-shaped cut into the side of England between Norfolk and Lincolnshire. Acres of tulips grow in the Fens around Spalding on the River Welland. Lying at the head of Scotia Creek which slices into the Wash's eastern shore is the market town and port of Boston – a stronghold of Puritanism in the 17th century.

The coastal regions of Lincolnshire were settled by Vikings from Scandinavia. The endings *-thorpe* and *-by* reveal the Viking origin of places such as Mablethorpe, Grimoldby and Spilsby. Skegness and other coastal towns are now popular seaside resorts. In 1936 Billy Butlin chose Ingoldmells for his first holiday camp.

Inland the rounded chalk hills of the Lincolnshire Wolds cut roughly north-south across the county. The Victorian poet Tennyson was born at Somersby on their eastern edge. Beyond them to the west Lincoln itself rises from a rocky hill, at the northern tip of Lincoln Edge, dominated by the three majestic towers of its great Norman cathedral – 'out and out the most precious piece of architecture in the British Isles,' in the opinion of the 19th-century art critic John Ruskin.

Smiling schoolchildren brandish miniature Union Jacks, perhaps to welcome a royal visitor. The British flag consists of three super-imposed crosses, reflecting the history of the nation: first, the red cross of St George (England's patron saint) on a white background; then the white diagonal cross of St Andrew (patron of Scotland) on a blue back-ground, added in 1707; finally, the diagonal cross of Ireland's St Patrick, again red on a white background.

Three industrial cities, each with a county attached, form a triangle in the east Midlands. Nottingham, in the north-east corner, is famous for lace, hosiery, bicycles and tobacco products. The appalling slums that surrounded the growing industrial cities of 19th-century England were notorious, and Nottingham had some of the worst. In parts 800 people were packed into filthy back-to-back housing covering one acre of ground.

Industry in the Midlands

Nottingham is regarded by many people as one of the most attractive cities in the Midlands. Traffic has been banned from much of its centre, which is presided over by the Castle, in fact a 17th-century mansion, rising from a crag above the River Trent. Each October most work comes to a halt for the three days of the Goose Fair – started in the Middle Ages, probably as a fair where geese were bought and sold before the feast of Michaelmas.

The remains of the royal forest of Sherwood stretch north from Nottingham in a thin ribbon. Sherwood is famous for the legendary outlaw and friend of the poor Robin Hood. Attempts have been made to identify him with a 12th-century Earl of Huntingdon, among others. But no one really knows who, if anyone, was the man behind the myth.

Rowing is an important part of the Oxbridge (Oxford and Cambridge) tradition, and the most famous sporting contest between the two universities is the annual Boat Race – rowed over a 4¹/2-mile stretch of the Thames in west London. Cambridge challenged Oxford to the first race in 1829 and until recently could claim the greater number of victories. Over the last decade, however, its star seems to have waned. Each university also has its own rowing events, such as the Cambridge 'Bumps' which take place in late February.

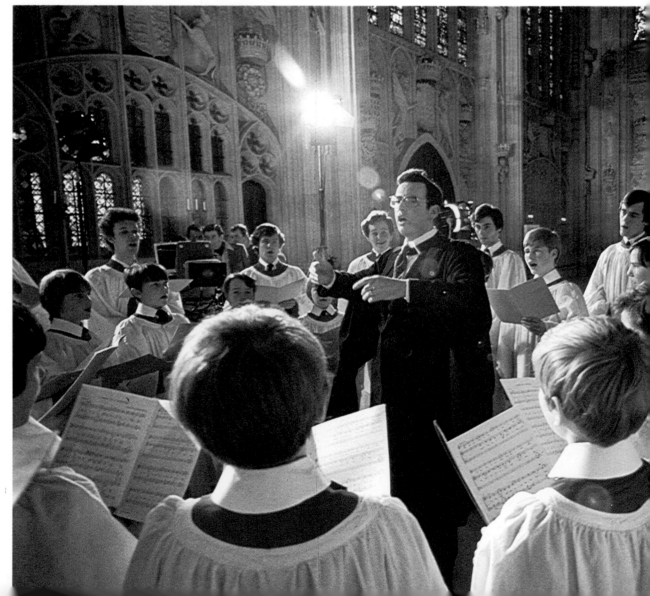

Resplendent in boater and blazer a young blood quaffs his pint as he watches the action at a rowing event. Upper-class Englishmen are not normally noted for their outrageous dress sense. But on occasions such as the Henley Royal Regatta they appear, with apparent equanimity, in the gaudiest of attire. Venerable old gentlemen sport lurid pink blazers with matching socks, the uniform of the elite Leander Club.

King's College Chapel, Cambridge is famous for its choir as well as its fine late medieval architecture. There are few more uplifting experiences than attending evensong at King's and listening to the voices of the boy sopranos echoing from the fan vaults above. King's has other claims to fame as well – the poet Rupert Brooke, the novelist E.M. Forster and the economist Maynard Keynes are just three of its former members.

Derby, west of Nottingham, boasts Britain's – and thus the world's – first factory, a water-powered silk-spinning mill built in 1717-21. Local products today include Crown Derby's beautiful blue-and-gold and red-and-gold porcelainware and Rolls-Royce aero engines.

Leicester forms the southern end of the triangle. Its chief industries are hosiery, textiles and engineering, while Melton Mowbray to the north-east is known for its pies and Stilton cheese. The dark orange Leicester cheese is a product of the county's rolling grasslands, which are also great fox-hunting territory.

Shoe-making has long been the staple industry of Northampton south of Leicester. Its county includes some of the most attractive scenery in the Midlands: open, rolling hills crisscrossed with dry-stone walls and dotted with towns such as Oundle and Stamford.

'One has no great hope of Birmingham. I always say there is something direful in the sound,' remarks Jane Austen's Mrs Elton in *Emma*. In fact, modern Britain's second largest city is a thriving and in many ways exciting place. Looking down on it from one of the many motorways that converge on the West Midlands (meeting at the aptly named 'Spaghetti Junction'), it seems a confusion of modern office blocks, factories and terraces of nondescript houses. Yet 'Brum' has much to offer. 'Brummies' are friendly and their city remains one of England's leading commercial and industrial centres. Birmingham has been spared the worst of the inner city misery and decay that afflicts many of England's other industrial centres. It is home to the huge modern National Exhibition Centre, has two universities, radio and television studios and one of England's best art galleries outside London.

The history of the West Midlands is marked by much that was best and worst about the Industrial Revolution.

Wolverhampton, which merges into Birmingham to the north-west, is a relatively prosperous place today, known for its locks and safes. In the 19th century, however, it was one of the living hells of the Industrial Revolution. It lies at the heart of the former coal and iron region known as the Black Country, whose furnaces and the dense palls of smoke they billowed forth created a landscape of despair. It was vividly described by Dickens in *The Old Curiosity Shop*: 'On every side, and as far as the eye could see into the heavy distance, tall chimneys ... poured out their plague of smoke, obscured the light, and made foul the melancholy air. On mounds of ashes by the wayside ... strange engines spun and writhed like tortured creatures; clanking their iron chains, shrieking in their rapid whirl from time to time as though in torment unendurable, and making the ground tremble with their agonies.'

Stratford-upon-Avon in Warwickshire south-east of Birmingham is devoted to the Shakespeare industry. The great dramatist and poet was born in Stratford in 1564, and in 1611 retired there having made a comfortable fortune from his plays. Stratford now makes a comfortable living from him. Tourists arrive by the coachload, wander around the streets and pleasant parks along the banks of the Avon, snap happily and perhaps attend a performance or two at the Royal Shakespeare Theatre (built in 1932) or the smaller Swan Theatre (1986).

North of Birmingham stretches the county of Stafford. A memorial in Stoke-on-Trent's church pays tribute to the great 18th-century porcelain maker Josiah Wedgwood, who 'converted a rude and inconsiderable manufactory into an elegant art and important part of the national commerce'. The region known as the Potteries, encompassing the five towns of Stoke-on-

Fox-hunting continues in most English shires, in spite of the activities of anti-blood sports campaigners and hunt saboteurs. Boxing Day is often the occasion for one of the season's most important meets. Riders, horses, hounds and the huntsmen in their traditional pink (actually red) gather outside a country pub or in the centre of a small market town, down a stirrup cup or two and then head out amidst the yelping of hounds for the chase.

A suitably rubicund farmer puts a magnificent draught horse through its paces at a country show. Though strictly redundant in the age of the tractor, the various draught breeds retain their place in the affections of many. A feature at some country shows is the horse-ploughing contest, where ploughmen are judged on the straight, clean finish of their furrows.

Trent, Tunstall, Burslem, Hanley and Longton, has been making pots since the Middle Ages. But Wedgwood transformed the business. A remarkable self-educated man of parts, who in later life regularly contributed articles to philosophical and antiquarian journals, he established his factory Etruria in 1769.

After the Potteries' industrial landscape come the rich

The North of England

The three counties of Yorkshire – formerly divided into three Ridings, from an Old English word meaning 'a third' – cover 4600 square miles, making them larger than Cyprus and over half the size of Wales. Indeed, they virtually form a nation of their own, as any good

dairy farming lands of Cheshire spreading out to the west. Fine black-and-white houses, notably Little Moreton Hall, rise in pretty country villages; rock salt is mined around Nantwich and Northwich, while Chester, lying near the mouth of the River Dee in the west and just a few miles from the Welsh border, is a popular shopping and tourist centre.

The industrial town of Macclesfield in east Cheshire lies on the edge of the Peak District. This wild and lovely region of moorlands, high crags and dales, rising to its highest point in Kinder Scout (or The Peak) at 2088 feet, is the southern end of the great Pennine range that stretches north as far as the Scottish borders.

Yorkshire person would hasten to agree. North Yorkshire alone stretches from the North Sea coast to within 12 miles of the west coast.

History and geography have combined to make Yorkshire – and the whole of the North – a very distinctive region of England. Unlike the people of the green and rolling south, Northerners have generally had to scratch a hard living in their beautiful but rarely fertile dales and fells. They also took much of the brunt of the misery as well as the prosperity of the Industrial Revolution. They are brisk, no-nonsense people with scant regard for pretension, often uncomfortably honest for the softer-spoken Southerners, but friendly.

Elegance as well as a love of music is the order of the evening at Glyndebourne in Sussex, where since 1934 the Christie family have held an annual opera festival in their small private opera house. The festival attracts some of the biggest names in the opera world, while for the audience an evening at Glyndebourne is an excuse for a picnic as well as a feast of music.

The ancient city of York, rising from the banks of the River Ouse in the Vale of York (one of the North's few fertile agricultural regions), has for centuries been regarded as the capital of the North. The Romans founded it as Eboracum in AD 71 and made it an important garrison town – Constantine the Great was first proclaimed emperor by his troops in York in 306. Under the Angles in 634 it became an archbishopric. Later the Vikings burnt the city, rebuilt it and temporarily renamed it Jorvik. It was an important railway town in the 19th century, but unlike many cities of the North never a major industrial centre, except for the manufacture of chocolate by Quaker families such as the Rowntrees and Terrys.

Today York has one of England's best universities, as well as being popular with shoppers and tourists. Walls, pierced by fortified gateways, still surround much of its centre; within them is a maze of streets (and a notoriously baffling one-way system) converging on the beautiful Minster, one of the finest Gothic cathedrals in Europe, the largest in northern Europe, famous also for its medieval stained-glass windows.

North Yorkshire represents Yorkshire's rural face. The flat lands of the Vale of York (really a northward extension of the Lincolnshire landscape) have many fine country houses, notably the baroque Castle Howard. The Vale is ringed by the ruins of great medieval abbeys: Rievaulx (pronounced 'Rivers'), Jervaulx and Fountains. Resort towns such as Scarborough and the old fishing port of Whitby line the North Sea coast, with the bleak but lovely North York Moors rising inland. Furrowing the eastern flank of the Pennines are the Yorkshire Dales: Swaledale, Wensleydale (famous for its cheese) and Wharfedale.

Yorkshire's industrial face is represented by West and South Yorkshire. Before the development of Boulton and Watt's steam engines, the streams and rivers tumbling down the Pennines' eastern side powered the mills of West Yorkshire's constellation of wool cities: the merging mass of Leeds and Bradford, with Halifax, Huddersfield and Wakefield to the south.

Wool brought West Yorkshire great wealth, reflected in its cities' fine civic buildings, such as Bradford's Wool Exchange and Leeds's magnificent classical Town Hall. Like many of the North's staple industries, wool has declined in the 20th century. On the whole, however, the West Yorkshire cities have met the challenge with some success. Leeds, for example, is now a major business and cultural centre.

Steel and coal brought South Yorkshire its industrial wealth. The billowing blast furnaces of Sheffield and Rotherham, tucked into the eastern Pennines, testify to their continuing importance as steel cities. Sheffield also has been famous for cutlery and Sheffield plate, a fusion of silver on copper, which was invented there in 1743. It still has Europe's largest manufacturers of household knives and similar products. To the north-east the Humber Estuary (spanned by the Humber

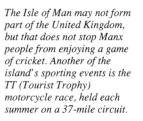

The Isle of Man may not form part of the United Kingdom, but that does not stop Manx people from enjoying a game of cricket. Another of the island's sporting events is the TT (Tourist Trophy) motorcycle race, held each summer on a 37-mile circuit.

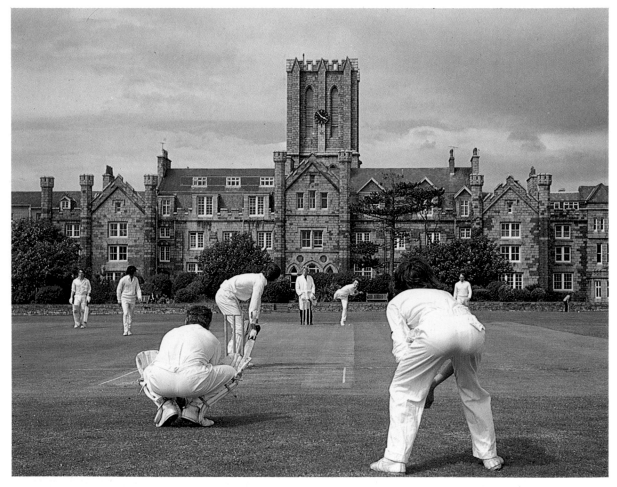

suspension bridge, opened in 1981, with the longest single span of any bridge in the world) forms a gash in the side of England. Hull (strictly Kingston upon Hull) on the Humber's north bank has been a major port since the 13th century and is growing once more in importance through increased trade with Europe. For most people Grimsby on the south bank is more or less synonymous with trawlers. It was once among the world's great fishing ports handling up to 200,000 tons of fish a year. Even today, its fish auctions held at 7.30 each morning are an impressive sight, with white-coated merchants bidding for slippery arrays of sole, turbot, halibut, cod and scallops.

North of Yorkshire the east coast closes in on the Pennines, leaving just narrow coastal strips between the mountains and the sea. The ancient city of Durham presents one of the most glorious sights in the North – its great Norman cathedral rising on a wooded bluff above a bend in the River Wear. Durham Castle, once seat of the powerful Prince-Bishops of Durham, is now part of the city's university. Durham's medieval quarter is an area of narrow streets and overhanging houses.

From Durham the Wear weaves its way north into the new county of Tyne and Wear. Newcastle upon Tyne was a great port long before the Industrial Revolution, shipping locally mined coal to London where it was known as 'sea coal' and used for household purposes – people already talked about 'taking coals to Newcastle' in the 17th century. It remains a fine city. Spanning the Tyne are three bridges, including Robert Stephenson's double-decker High Level Bridge with one tier for trains and another for motor traffic.

And yet, for all Newcastle's glories, Tyneside as a whole and the city of Sunderland at the mouth of the Wear to the south are among the most depressed regions in England, indeed in western Europe. Apart from coal, shipbuilding was the chief industry of Tyne and Wear. At the turn of the century shipyards lined the banks of the Tyne from Newcastle to Tynemouth to the north and from Gateshead through Jarrow to South Shields to the south, while Sunderland was reckoned to be the world's greatest shipbuilding centre. The new century was, however, to bring acute misery to the region. Depression resulted in high unemployment in the 1930s and decline in the 1980s and 90s, with the added pressure of competition from the shipyards of the Far East.

In welcome contrast to the urban jungle and despair of much of Tyneside come the open spaces of Northumberland, one of the loneliest and loveliest landscapes in England. Sandy beaches backed by grass-covered dunes stretch for miles along the shores of bays such as Embleton Bay. The River Aln leads to Alnwick whose castle is the seat of the historic Percy family, Dukes of Northumberland. To the north, grey seals come ashore on the Farne Islands to breed, and thousands of sea birds nest there each year. Longstone lighthouse was the home of the heroine Grace Darling who on a stormy night in 1838 rowed out with her father through towering waves to rescue nine men aboard the stricken steamer *Forfarshire*. Lindisfarne is an ancient seat of Christianity where in the 7th century Saints Aidan and Cuthbert were priors of the now ruined monastery.

Inland meanwhile stretch huge expanses of sheep-grazed moorland. The remains of Hadrian's Wall built to guard the northernmost frontier of the Roman Empire stride across the southern portion of the county. Further north the Cheviot Hills mark the modern border with Scotland. Until James VI of Scotland became James I of England in 1603, this was a region of near incessant warfare between the two nations. What is now England's northernmost town, Berwick-upon-Tweed, changed hands no fewer than thirteen times before finally falling to the English in 1482.

It was the relative dampness of their climate that helped to make the fortunes of the great cotton towns of Burnley, Manchester, Oldham, Rochdale, Bury, Bolton and Blackburn in the western Pennines. From the 1780s onwards Manchester, in particular, grew from a modest town to one of the greatest cities of industrial England.

Manchester was more than just an industrial centre, however. It rapidly acquired an intellectual tradition. 'What Manchester thinks one day, London thinks the next,' Mancunians used to boast. Some of Victorian Britain's leading liberal politicians and economists, such as Richard Cobden and John Bright, were members of the 'Manchester School'. At the same time, however, the squalor of the Manchester slums had a profound effect on another political and economic thinker, Karl Marx's associate Friedrich Engels, who for many years ran the Manchester end of his family's textile business. His book *The Condition of the Working Class in England*, published in 1845, was based on observations of the Manchester slums and became a key text of early Communism.

The Manchester Ship Canal, built in 1894, links the city with the Mersey Estuary and Liverpool. If Manchester has survived the decline of its traditional industry with some success, Liverpool has been less fortunate. The great port whose docks in 1880 stretched for seven miles along the banks of the Mersey and whose ships carried 40 per cent of the world's trade has suffered a dramatic decline since the Second World War. Its docks are now mostly empty and decaying, and unemployment is among the highest in Britain. For much of the 1980s and into the 90s its city council has been wracked by regular financial crises and bouts of in-fighting among left-wing factions.

And yet for all their city's decay, the 'Scouses', as the natives of Liverpool call themselves, have a special vitality. It was Liverpool, after all, that produced the Beatles. John Lennon, Paul McCartney, George Harrison and Ringo Starr were all born there and established their careers in the city's Cavern Club.

Liverpool is also a point for ferries plying across the Irish Sea to one of Britain's constitutional anomalies – the Isle of Man which, though a dependency of the British Crown, is not part of the United Kingdom. It has its own parliament, the Court of Tynwald, which includes a representative assembly, the House of Keys.

Back on the mainland Lancashire has long been

The English are justly
famous for their love of
gardening. In the country,
cottage gardens have
carefully tended flower and
vegetable beds. The most
hotly contested competitions
at country shows are those
for the best roses, best
dahlias, biggest marrow
and so on.

A fly-fisherman casts his
line across the trout-filled
waters of a lake on
Dartmoor. Forests still
cover parts of the moor,
which is now a national
park spreading out over 400
square miles. The rest is
open moorland, rocky
outcrops or 'tors' with the
occasional treacherous bog.
Dartmoor was the setting
for Conan Doyle's Sherlock
Holmes tale, The Hound of
the Baskervilles. It is also
the real-life setting for
Dartmoor Prison, which
was opened in 1809,
originally to house French
prisoners of the Napoleonic
Wars.

copper once mined on Dartmoor underpinned the rise of ports such as Plymouth, Dartmouth and Exeter on the south coast and Barnstable on the north coast. And the booty brought home by the great Elizabethan sea dogs added to the county's prosperity. As in Cornwall, the railways brought tourists in large numbers to the county – and they still come. Imposing Victorian and Edwardian hotels continue to do a thriving business along the clifftops of south coast resorts from Salcombe in the west to Sidmouth in the east. Along the north coast, visitors are drawn by the enduring picture-postcard quaintness of places such as Clovelly, Ilfracombe and Lynmouth.

As Devon gives way to Dorset, the coastline changes yet again. High white chalk cliffs replace the red marl

Cricket is, without doubt, the most typically English of games, but it is also a hugely popular sport in former colonies such as the West Indies, India and Australia. It is by far the most difficult of sports for the uninitiated spectator to understand. Its origins are obscure, but it has probably been played for about 400 years.

headlands. Resorts continue to dot the shore, but these are resorts with a Georgian and Regency elegance that pre-dates the railway era. Lyme Regis, a few miles east of the Devon border, was popular in the age of Jane Austen, and at Weymouth, to the east, King George III became in 1789 the first British monarch to use a bathing machine.

Inland, Dorset is a beautiful county of open chalk downlands, where in season vast acres of barley sway in the wind. Its ways and landscape were chronicled in loving detail, though with a bleak pessimism, by the novelist Thomas Hardy, born in 1840 at Higher Bockhampton, near the county town of Dorchester (Casterbridge in his novels).

A region of gentle hills runs along north Dorset's border with Somerset, and beyond them lie the flat and strangely eerie peatlands of the Somerset Levels, interrupted by the occasional wooded hillock and crisscrossed by narrow drainage canals, or 'rhines'. The region used to be famous for its apple orchards, and still makes cider (or 'zider' in the Somerset dialect) and a particularly lethal local version of it, known as scrumpy.

Once the Levels were salt marshes, and the area around Glastonbury to the north of Sedgemoor (the site, in 1685, of the last battle on English soil) was an island rising from the marshes. It is a place steeped in legend. Joseph of Arimathea is said to have come to Glastonbury after the Crucifixion to establish the first Christian church in England. On his arrival, legend tells, he struck his staff into the ground and it promptly sprouted twigs and blossomed – hence the famous Glastonbury Thorn which to this day blossoms around Christmas. Other legends identify Glastonbury with the Isle of Avalon where King Arthur came to die.

Avon is dominated by the twin cities of Bath and Bristol. Bath, set in the deep valley of the Avon river, is one of England's great tourist cities, along with Oxford, Cambridge and Stratford-upon-Avon. It is famous for the glories of its Regency architecture and the mineral waters that made it the most fashionable spa in Georgian England. But it would be a busy place even without the tourists, for it is also the major shopping centre in the West of England.

Bath grew from its spa waters. Bristol grew from a rather dirtier trade – that of human flesh. In the 18th century it was the principal English corner of the triangular slave trade that plied between England, West Africa and the West Indies. It also has strong links with the pioneering Victorian engineer Isambard Kingdom Brunel. His Great Western Railway first ran from London to Bristol, and the Clifton suspension bridge, spanning the rocky heights of the Avon Gorge, was built to his design.

In the early 20th century the port of Bristol declined as ships became too large to reach it up the Avon (Avonmouth, to the west, has replaced it as the West Country's chief port). But Bristol remains a flourishing place, with an important university, the well-known Bristol Old Vic theatre company and plenty of industry – food, drink, tobacco, paper and aircraft among others.

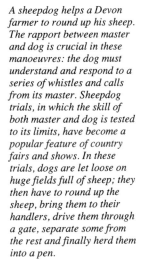

A sheepdog helps a Devon farmer to round up his sheep. The rapport between master and dog is crucial in these manoeuvres: the dog must understand and respond to a series of whistles and calls from its master. Sheepdog trials, in which the skill of both master and dog is tested to its limits, have become a popular feature of country fairs and shows. In these trials, dogs are let loose on huge fields full of sheep; they then have to round up the sheep, bring them to their handlers, drive them through a gate, separate some from the rest and finally herd them into a pen.

The Northern Kingdom

When James VI of Scotland became James I of England after the death of his cousin Queen Elizabeth in 1603, he was quite clear in his own mind what this meant. After centuries of warfare, or at best uneasy truces, the two kingdoms were now finally to be merged into an indissoluble unit. Addressing the English Parliament in characteristically flowery terms the following year, he pronounced: 'I am the Husband and the whole Isle is my lawfull Wife; I am the Head; and it is my Body ... I hope therefore no man will be so unreasonable as to think that I, that am a Christian King under the Gospel, should be a polygamist and husband to two wives; that I being the Head should have a divided and monstrous Body.'

When the Scottish National Party met for its annual conference in September 1991, one slogan in particular fired the enthusiasm of its delegates: 'Scotland free in 93'. For nearly 400 years Scotland and England have shared one monarch; since the Act of Union in 1707 they have shared one parliament, meeting at Westminster. Yet many Scots still regard themselves as part of an entirely separate nation. A minority favours outright independence, and many more aspire to at least some measure of autonomy.

The Scots are a gritty, determined people – they have had to be. Beneath all the encrustations of myth and romance that are commonly associated with their beautiful country lies a history of exceptional turbulence. The stories of figures such as Mary Queen of Scots and Bonnie Prince Charlie are romantic and appealing, but a backdrop of raw violence rises behind them. Mary Queen of Scots, for example, was to a large extent a victim of the bitter religious divisions that wracked Scotland in the 16th century, and Bonnie Prince Charlie's failed rebellion of 1745-6 ended in the brutal 'pacification' of the Highlands by the Hanoverian Duke of Cumberland. Even the glorious loneliness of the Highlands' wonderful landscape of loch, moor and mountain is largely a product of the 'Clearances' of the 18th and 19th centuries, when thousands of peasant crofters were forced off their traditional lands by former clan chieftains anxious to make a quick profit from the raising of sheep.

Turbulent as the Scots' history has been, however, it has not damped their special genius. There is a paradox in their character: on the one hand, the Celtic romance; on the other, the often puritanical strictness associated

Scotland's tartan pageantry is largely an invention of the Victorians. From as early as Roman times the people of Caledonia (Scotland) were known for their 'chequered garments', but the particular patterns people wore had little real significance. Then came the romantic, 19th-century enthusiasm for things Scottish. The few genuinely ancient clan tartans were added to by haberdashers eager to invent new patterns for clients with any claim to Scottish ancestry. Today's array of tartans – many strikingly attractive – include separate hunting and dress 'sets' for the different clans, regimental sets, regional sets, and even a special set for clergymen.

The 'Glorious Twelfth' of August is an important date in the sportsman's calendar. It marks the beginning of the grouse-shooting season. The 19th century saw huge areas of the Highlands given over to sporting estates where red deer were stalked, salmon caught, and grouse, blackcock and capercaillie shot. It was, and still is, sport for wealthy outsiders, however. Locals may find employment as 'gillies', guides and attendants to the sportsmen, but otherwise reap little benefit from the estates.

with the Presbyterian kirk. The Scots seem to be able to combine hard-headed common sense with romantic dash and flair, a remarkably fruitful combination which has yielded more than its fair share of outstanding people. In the fields of science and engineering alone, Scotland has produced figures as diverse as John McAdam, the road-builder who gave his name to Tarmac; the Scottish-born inventor of the telephone, Alexander Graham Bell; the 19th-century physicist, James Clerk Maxwell, whose theoretical work in magnetism prepared the way for wireless telegraphy; and James Watt, who developed the steam engine, the workhorse of the Industrial Revolution.

In the circumstances it is hardly surprising that the Scots have clung so tenaciously, and so successfully, to their national identity. In fact, the Act of Union did leave them with certain areas of autonomy. They have their own established Presbyterian kirk and their own legal and educational systems. But the last few decades have seen an upsurge in demands for much greater independence. In 1967 many political pundits were taken by surprise when a nationalist candidate won a Labour seat in a by-election at Hamilton just outside Glasgow. By 1974 the Scottish National Party (SNP) were fielding 11 MPs in the House of Commons. The discovery of oil in Scottish North Sea waters from 1969 onwards gave rise to new hopes, and new resentments – hopes that oil revenues would give Scotland a real chance to stand on its own economically, resentments that the revenues were channelled to Westminster.

A referendum in 1979 revealed that a majority of Scots favoured the devolution of significant powers from Westminster to an elected assembly in Edinburgh. The majority (52 per cent) fell short, however, of the margin needed to trigger the necessary changes. During the following decade many Scots felt growing resentment that a country which in 1987 elected only ten Conservative MPs in 72 constituencies should be shackled with what they regarded as an unsympathetic Conservative government in London. In nationalist circles the idea of independence within the European Community – a 'Europe of the regions' – became increasingly popular. Admittedly, support for the SNP (in spite of the eye-catching endorsement of the actor Sean Connery) ran at just 19 per cent in September 1991. But by then two of Britain's three main political parties, the Liberal Democrats and Labour (who in 1987 won 50 of the Scottish seats), had committed themselves to establishing an Edinburgh assembly. The tide in favour of constitutional change seemed to be flowing strongly.

The thistle – one of Scotland's two chief emblems, along with the diagonal cross of St Andrew – is a reminder of Viking invaders who ruled large parts of the country for many centuries. Legend has it that before the Battle of Largs (fought on the shores of the Firth of Clyde in 1263) a barefoot Viking warrior, creeping up on the Scottish army as part of a surprise attack, stepped on a thistle and let out a loud cry that alerted the Scots to their danger. They went on to defeat the Vikings and drive them out of much of their land.

The ruins of Dunnottar Castle rise dramatically from a headland on Scotland's east coast. Here, in 1651, the Honours of Scotland (its crown jewels) were brought for safe keeping from invading English troops under Oliver Cromwell. The castle eventually fell to Cromwell's men but, according to one story, not before the Honours had been smuggled out in a basket of flax.

Border warfare

Narrow streets and high stone houses roofed with grey tiles characterise many Border towns such as Jedburgh. An atmosphere of quiet prosperity prevails – a far cry from the days of more-or-less incessant Border warfare across the region that only came to an end with the union of the crowns of Scotland and England in 1603.

To a large extent the romantic image of Scotland is due to one man: the writer Sir Walter Scott, whose splendidly turreted home, Abbotsford (model for many later mock-baronial castles in Scotland), rises near the banks of the River Tweed in the Borders. He was a great man and a great writer, certainly in his earlier works. From 1814 he published a series of enormously popular novels – the so-called *Waverley* novels, after the title of the first – which, with remarkable balance and accuracy, explored for the first time the key themes of Scottish history. Sadly, financial pressures in later life forced him to churn out a succession of potboilers which were little more than romantic adventure yarns. And it was from these that the sentimental Victorian and Hollywood views of Scotland were quarried – a sad injustice to the memory of a man who had a sure grasp of his country's character and history, its dour and violent side as well as its romance.

Although Scott was born in Edinburgh, his family came from the Borders of southern Scotland and he spent much of his childhood there. In this he was fortunate, for the Borders are among Scotland's loveliest regions. The Lammermuir and Moorfoot Hills covered with rough moorland, line their northern edge, and the higher Tweedsmuirs (where another great adventure writer, John Buchan, had his roots) rise in the south-west. The Lauderdale, Tweed and Teviot rivers carve their way through the hills, meeting in the rich flat farming lands of The Merse near the North Sea coast. Towns such as Galashiels and Hawick are centres of the Border tweed industry. Set among the hills are many fine country houses, including Traquair House (claiming to be the oldest inhabited house in Scotland, parts of it dating from the early 13th century) and Mellerstain, designed by the father-and-son team of William and Robert Adam between 1725 and 1778. It is also great horse country. Towns such as Lanark and Peebles have annual Common Riding festivals when hundreds of horsemen and women turn out to beat the bounds of the towns' ancient common lands. Sometimes there is also a costumed re-enactment of a local medieval battle.

And yet, tranquil as they are now, the Borders have one of the bloodiest histories of any region in Scotland. For centuries wars between the Scots and English raged back and forth across these lovely hills. The ruins of the four great abbeys at Kelso, Jedburgh, Melrose and Dryburgh bear witness to the violence of those times. Founded in the 12th century by the devout and (paradoxically) anglicised Scottish King David I, not one survives intact. All were brought to ruin at one point or another by English armies. In 1545 Kelso Abbey became a temporary fortress defended by 100 local men, including 12 monks. All were slaughtered when the English finally stormed the abbey, destroying most of it in the process.

Not that the fault lay entirely with the English. A group of unruly clans, including the Homes, Kerrs and Scotts, dominated the Scottish side of the Border lands.

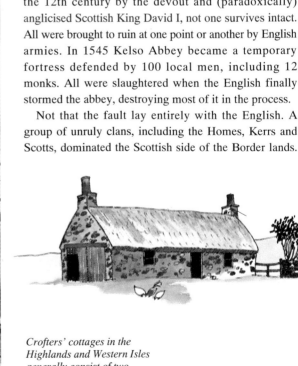

Crofters' cottages in the Highlands and Western Isles generally consist of two rooms heated by peat fires.

When times were hard they would form bands of mosstroopers or reivers who sallied forth into Northumberland, returning with flocks of English sheep or herds of English cattle to replenish their stocks. Many of their exploits are recounted in the various Border ballads. One larger-scale Border raid, which culminated in the Battle of Otterburn of 1388, is recorded in two ballads, one English, one Scottish: the Northumberland ballad *Chevvy Chase,* and the Border ballad *The Battle of Otterbourne,* which describes the gathering of the raiding party led by the 'doughty' Lord Douglas, Douglas's death at the hands of the English Percy (Shakespeare's Harry Hotspur), and the subsequent victory of the Scottish, despite their leader's death, with 'the Percy led captive away'.

Bid for freedom

The respective fortunes of the Scots and English waxed and waned a great deal. David I, for example, who reigned from 1124 to 1153, was effective ruler of huge areas of northern England. Some 150 years later,

however, the boot was firmly on the other foot. In 1296 Edward I of England, the 'Hammer of the Scots', invaded Scotland, declared himself feudal overlord and appointed an English governor to rule in his name. In a final humiliating stroke, he also carried off the Stone of Destiny upon which the Scottish kings were traditionally crowned at Scone in central Scotland. A rebellion led by Sir William Wallace had some initial success in 1297 but was defeated by Edward the following year at Falkirk, west of Edinburgh. Wallace escaped, only to be betrayed in 1305 and taken to London, where he was tried and gruesomely hanged and quartered as a traitor.

The following year, a group of Scottish patriots met secretly in a church at Dumfries in the south-west of the country. They included Robert Bruce, related to the former Scottish royal house, and John Comyn – 'the Red' – representing the powerful Balliol family, also with royal connections. It was a stormy meeting. Robert Bruce (later to become one of the great heroes of Scottish history) suspected Comyn of treachery and finally, in a moment of rage, stabbed him. Aghast, he apparently rushed out of the church crying, 'I doubt I have slain the Comyn.' A faithful henchman

Three stern-faced peat cutters lean for a rest against a pile of peat briquettes. Peat bogs cover large areas of the northern Highlands and islands. Peat is exported for gardening purposes and briquettes are used as a household fuel. There was even an experiment in Caithness in the far north to use peat in the generation of electricity.

replied, 'I'll make siccar [sure],' and went in to complete the job.

Shortly afterwards Robert Bruce proclaimed himself king of Scotland and was crowned at Scone. But he had little initial success. Within the space of a few months he was defeated by the English, excommunicated by the church for his 'sacrilegious' murder of Comyn, and his wife and daughter were taken hostage. At this point, according to legend, he went into hiding, living in a cave on the island of Rathlin off the Irish coast, where he was inspired by the persistence of a spider climbing up the side of the cave. Whatever the truth of this story, Bruce did persist, and early in 1307 made a comeback in the west of Scotland. In July, came the welcome news of Edward I's death. Bruce, having first spent seven years securing his

Sheep have rather unhappy associations in the Highlands. In the 19th century many crofters were driven from their traditional lands by landlords, or 'lairds', who were keen to give their estates over to the more profitable grazing of sheep. The empty landscape of the modern Highlands, so attractive to tourists, was one of the results of these often brutal Clearances.

The dark face and curled horns are the distinguishing characteristics of the Scottish Blackface sheep, the staple breed of the Highlands. They are chiefly raised for meat, their wool being too coarse for clothing, though some is used in carpet-making. Scottish sheep also provide the ingredients of the traditional delicacy, haggis. This is made from a gruesome mix of the minced heart, lungs and liver of a sheep, mingled with suet, onions and oatmeal.

West Highland cattle lend an added shaggy splendour to Glen Nevis. On the left rise the lower slopes of Ben Nevis, at 4406 feet Britain's highest mountain. The glen – one of the wildest and loveliest in the Highlands – was once home to a branch of the Cameron clan, who during the Jacobite rebellion of 1745 led an unsuccessful attempt to capture neighbouring Fort William from government troops.

Sadly, West Highland cattle – the closest surviving descendants of the original wild cattle of Britain – are an increasingly rare sight in their native landscape. They are extremely hardy and their meat is excellent, but they take longer to mature than more modern breeds and yield less meat. In north-eastern Scotland the huge, black Aberdeen Angus continues to be an important beef breed.

claim to the throne against his rivals – including the Comyn family – went on to defeat the English at Bannockburn near Stirling in 1314. He ruled Scotland until his death, possibly from leprosy, in 1329. In accordance with his dying wishes, his heart was taken on pilgrimage before, it is believed, being buried at Melrose Abbey.

Dumfries, where Bruce slew 'Red' Comyn, stands in the region of Dumfries and Galloway, the bulge of Scotland that protrudes west of the Borders towards Ireland. Lying well off the main routes to the north, it is something of a forgotten region for many outsiders. It is attractive for all that. A series of river estuaries indent the south coast, with towns such as Kirkcudbright (pronounced 'K'coobri') and Wigtown, as well as Dumfries, at their heads. At its western end is the T-shaped peninsula called The Rhins of Galloway, with the port of Stranraer sheltering at the head of Loch Ryan – from where ferries cross to Northern Ireland. The

As in England, the pub holds a sacred place in Scottish communities. The Scots may be staunch Presbyterians but that does not prevent many of them from being strong imbibers as well. Glaswegians in particular enjoy a 'wee hauf and hauf' – a tot of whisky chased down by half a pint of beer.

The characteristic high tenement buildings of Edinburgh's Old Town rise above Princes Street Gardens. In the centre are the twin towers of the Assembly Hall, where the Church of Scotland holds its annual General Assembly.

high society, he returned to Galloway, eventually taking up a post as an exciseman in Dumfries. He died in Dumfries in 1796, aged 37, his health having been ruined by drink.

For all his difficulties, Burns kept an impish zest for life that has ever since endeared him to the Scots. Burns Night, the anniversary of his birth on January 25, is celebrated each year as one of Scotland's best-loved festivals. Families meet together for a meal of haggis – Scotland's national dish – served with *chappit tatties* (potatoes) and *bashed neeps* (mashed swedes), all washed down with plenty of whisky. The feasters traditionally read out the poet's *Address to a Haggis* and start the meal with his *Selkirk Grace*:

> Some hae meat and canna eat,
> And some wad eat that want it;
> But we hae meat and we can eat,
> Sae let the Lord be thankit.

Wigtown, which lies to the west of Dumfries, brings a reminder of the other side of the Scottish character – a memorial behind the town on Windyhill commemorating the Wigtown Martyrs. The 1680s have gone down in Scottish history as the 'Killing Times', an episode that has its roots in the two Covenants signed by Scottish Presbyterian leaders in 1638 and 1643. By these the 'Covenanters' sought to uphold the strict precepts of their own church, including a refusal to countenance either bishops or the Anglican Prayer Book which Charles I was attempting to impose. During the ascendancy of the puritans under Oliver Cromwell they had largely like-minded neighbours to the south, but then came the Restoration of Charles II in 1660. The new authorities were determined to force both bishops

A shop window displays numerous brands of Scotland's most famous drink. Scotch whisky has two forms: malt whisky, made using malted barley (barley that has been allowed to ferment), and grain whisky, which is distilled from malted and unmalted barley. Pure malt whisky (especially 'single malt' coming from one distillery) is regarded as a particularly fine drink. Most of the commonly drunk brands are blends of both malt and grain whisky.

north-west coast is more frequented, lined with numerous golf courses and resort towns such as Ayr and Wemyss Bay, which are popular with Glaswegians when they go 'doon the watter' during their Fair Fortnight each July.

Galloway is Burns country. Scotland's favourite poet Robert Burns, author of *Auld Lang Syne,* was born at Alloway near Ayr in 1759. His life was far from easy. He early acquired a habit of hard drinking and a series of farming ventures all failed. In a moment of complete desperation in his late twenties he decided to emigrate to Jamaica in the West Indies to work as a bookkeeper on a sugar estate. It was then that he published his first collection of poems, hoping to raise the money for his passage. It proved a turning point. The poems were an immediate success and he was able to stay in Scotland. After a period in Edinburgh, where he was lionised by

and the Prayer Book on the Scottish kirk. Some people acquiesced, others refused. Groups of these 'Covenanters' rebelled in 1666 and again in 1679, and were twice defeated. The 'Killing Times' followed, with anyone suspected of Covenanting sympathies hunted down and executed. It is a story of extraordinary fanaticism on both sides. Scores around Wigtown alone met their deaths. Perhaps the most poignant episode is of two women, one a girl of 18, the other a widow of 63. They were tied to stakes on the Wigtown salt marshes and then, refusing to the last to renounce their religious beliefs, left to drown as the tide came in.

Northern capital

No amount of lowering grey weather, drizzling Scotch mist or bitter wind whipping through the streets from the North Sea can detract from Edinburgh's charm. Scotland's capital is scarcely blessed by its climate, but in every other way it is unquestionably one of the most beautiful cities in Britain, if not in Europe. Not even Bath, in England, can match the Georgian glories of its New Town, while in setting it has few equals. Perched on a series of ridges to the south of the Firth of Forth, overlooked from a crag by its castle, with the green,

The islands of Shetland are famous for their patterned knitwear. Traditionally, Shetlanders pluck, or roo, *rather than shear the wool from their sheep. The wool of the Shetland sheep is exceptionally fine and soft.*

Scotland has two main tweed-producing regions. Harris tweed is hand-woven (as seen here) in the Outer Hebrides. Border tweed is manufactured in small mills in the Border towns.

Originally, the fabric was known as 'tweel', but a London cloth merchant, thinking of the River Tweed in the Borders, mistook the word for 'tweed' and the name has stuck.

When you can't wear the full Highland outfit of kilt, sporran and the rest, you can at least show your allegiances with a Highland bonnet and tartan scarf. Although most of the Highland costume owes more to 19th-century romantics than to anything worn by the clansmen of old, it has put down deep roots in the affections of the Scots, particularly perhaps the 'exiled' Scots of places such as North America, Australia and South Africa.

The first stage in the making of whisky is to soak the barley for up to three days in tanks of the soft, peaty water of the whisky regions. After soaking, the barley grains are spread out in concrete-floored buildings such as this and left to germinate for up to 12 days. The malt is then dried in kilns, ground and mixed with hot water.

formerly volcanic mound of Arthur's Seat to the east, it enjoys all the drama the Scottish landscape can lend it.

Central Edinburgh has two distinct halves. The Old Town – the original heart of the city – covers the ridge that stretches from the castle to the northern slopes of Arthur's Seat, with the series of streets known as the Royal Mile (and indeed roughly a mile in length) running along its spine. High tenement buildings topped with crow-stepped gables, typical of pre-Georgian

Scottish town architecture, line narrow streets with even narrower wynds (alleys) leading off them. When the New Town was started in the late 18th century, most of Edinburgh's wealthier citizens left the Old Town, preferring the openness and space of the new terraces and crescents. In recent years, however, many young professionals have been rediscovering the historic charms of the Old Town and the area is in the process of 're-gentrification'.

The New Town is the result of a competition. In 1767 the city authorities decided that the capital needed to be expanded and, in a way that has now become familiar, invited architects to submit plans for how it should be done. The winner was the 27-year-old James Craig. The heart of the New Town – the rectangular grid of streets spreading over the ridge which runs parallel with the Old Town to the north – was built according to his plans. The New Town is now Edinburgh's commercial and professional centre. Shoppers scurry along Princes Street, overlooked by the castle to the south, and dip into department stores such as Jenners, while suited money-men hurry to work in the banks and finance houses of Charlotte Square, Edinburgh's miniature version of the City of London.

A liquid, known as 'wort', is extracted and yeast added. This is then transferred to the stills for the distillation process. The stills are kept going night and day, and the peat fires that heat them must never be allowed to go out. Unlike Irish whiskey, which is distilled three times, Scotch whisky is distilled only twice. Finally, the whisky is left to mellow for at least three years in oak casks.

At the same time as Edinburgh's architectural renewal came an extraordinary cultural and intellectual blossoming which earned the city the title of the 'Athens of the North'. During the late 18th and 19th centuries it was home to talents as widely varied as those of Sir Walter Scott, the philosopher David Hume, the economist Adam Smith, the painter Allan Ramsay, and the writer Robert Louis Stevenson. Its university, founded in 1582, was particularly famous for its medical school – it was in Edinburgh in 1847 that chloroform was first used. One medical student was the young Arthur Conan Doyle, who is said to have based Sherlock Holmes on one of his lecturers. Since 1947 the Edinburgh International Festival of Music and Drama has been one of Europe's liveliest cultural feasts. During August and September, the Festival with its attendant Fringe fills every available theatre, church hall, school gymnasium, basement, even many pavements with performers and audiences from all over the world.

The 19th-century novelist Charlotte Brontë remarked that 'Edinburgh compared to London is like a vivid page of history compared to a huge dull treatise on political economy'. Certainly, Edinburgh is refreshingly compact and also steeped in history. A walk along the Royal Mile is like a stroll through the most notable episodes of Scotland's past. The castle itself brings reminders of the origins of the capital.

It was the early Pictish peoples of Scotland who first built a fort here called Duneadain – 'fort on a slope'. When Angles from Northumberland ruled much of this region, one of their kings, Edwin, adapted the original name to Edwin's Burgh. The present castle dates mostly from the 14th century. In 1566 Mary Queen of Scots gave birth to her son, later James VI of Scotland and James I of England, within its grim walls.

From the castle, Lawnmarket leads to Parliament Square, which is dominated by the Gothic High Kirk of Edinburgh (often incorrectly known as St Giles' Cathedral). From 1560 to 1572 the great leader of the Scottish Reformation, John Knox, was Edinburgh's

Knowing when the whisky has distilled to perfection is part of the whisky-maker's art. Modern scientific methods help but are no substitute for the instinct and flair of the expert distiller.

minister. His reputation has been much maligned. He was opinionated, stubborn and unafraid of anybody, yet at the same time he could be gently humorous and had a deep concern for the poor. He was also an inspirational preacher, which often led to trouble when people took his words more literally than he intended. He was one of the preachers whose sermons against idolatry led to the despoiling of Perth's religious houses in May 1559. He also believed that to promote a woman to any form of rule was the 'subversion of good order, of all equality and justice'. One of his earliest publications was a pamphlet luridly entitled *First Blast of the Trumpet against the Monstrous Regiment of Women*, which was an attack on the Catholic Queen Mary I of England, among others.

Adjoining the High Kirk is the Parliament House, which, since the demise of the Scottish Parliament in 1707, has housed Scotland's highest courts of justice. Wigged advocates (roughly equivalent to barristers) and writers (solicitors) hurry to court through the Gothic Parliament Hall. Scottish law is more akin to Continental than to English law, in that it appeals to

codified principles of justice (inspired in part by Roman law) rather than precedent. It also has three possible verdicts: guilty, not guilty and not proven – which means that the defendant can be brought back to trial if new evidence emerges.

From Parliament Square the Royal Mile leads along High Street and Cannongate to the elaborate wrought-iron gates of the Palace of Holyroodhouse, the Queen's official residence in Scotland. Most of the present palace dates from the Restoration, but the earlier north-west corner, with its memories of Mary Queen of Scots,

survives. The tower contains the few private rooms where the attractive, vivacious and talented 19-year-old Queen – of whom Knox was forced grudgingly to admit that she seemed to have 'some inchantment whareby men ar betwitched' – made her home when she returned to a troubled Scotland in 1561.

Aged just six days, she had become Queen on the death of her father James V after a massive defeat at the hands of the English. This was at the height of the Auld Alliance by which the Scottish rulers sought to counterbalance the weight of their ever-encroaching neighbour to the south through strong ties with France. The infant Queen was sent to France, where she eventually married the dauphin, later Francis II. When the sickly Francis died in 1560 she had no option but to return to her northern kingdom.

Scotland was in the throes of its Reformation, with the Protestants led by Knox very much in the ascendant. Mary, a devout Catholic, insisted on her right to attend Mass in the privacy of Holyrood. This, however, was too much for the Reformers and brought the first major conflict of her seven years in Scotland. In a series of interviews, held in Holyrood's Audience Chamber, Knox harangued the unfortunate Queen, who at first

North Atlantic waves make little impression on the 1000-foot sandstone cliffs of Hoy (its name coming from the Norse for 'high island') in the islands of Orkney. Near Hoy's western tip is the isolated, 450-ft stack known as the Old Man of Hoy, first climbed in 1966. The island also forms the high south-western shore of Scapa Flow, one of the finest natural harbours in the world and a vital naval anchorage in both World Wars. In 1919 the captured German fleet scuttled itself in Scapa Flow rather than fall into British hands. Seven of the 74 ships sunk still lie below the surface and thousands of divers come to explore them each year.

tried to reason with him but finally lost her patience: 'I have borne with you in all your rigorous manner of speaking ... I offered unto you presence and audience, whensoever it pleased you to admonishe me, and yet I cannot be quit of you; I vow to God I shall be once revenged.'

In 1565 Mary married a second time, to her decorative but weak-minded cousin, the Earl of Darnley – a Catholic. The marriage was a disaster. Darnley's tiresome ambitions alienated the Queen's wiser counsellors, and fairly promptly the Queen herself, who came to spend more and more time with an Italian

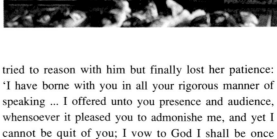

Gulls take what pickings they can find in Aberdeen's covered fish market. The 'Granite City' on Scotland's east coast is a fishing port and has thrived since the 1970s as the headquarters and transport centre for the North Sea oil industry. It also has a university, founded before 1500, and three cathedrals. The poet Lord Byron spent much of his childhood in Aberdeen, his mother coming from an ancient local family, the Gordons of Gight.

A Highland lass looks down pensively during a regional gathering. The elaboration of Highland costume during the 19th century included special adaptations for women. For young girls, their outfit is more or less the same as for boys and men: kilt, cutaway jacket and bonnet. At more formal events, such as Highland balls, the women often wear a white or plain long dress with a tartan sash.

musician (later promoted to the Queen's secretary), David Rizzio. Darnley grew jealous and in March 1566 Rizzio was murdered inside the private apartments at Holyrood, possibly in the Queen's presence. Mary then fell under the influence of the Protestant Earl of Bothwell, while Darnley was banished to a house in Edinburgh known as Kirk o'Field. One night in February 1567 Kirk o'Field was mysteriously blown up and the body of Darnley found strangled in a nearby garden. Bothwell was clearly implicated in the murder, though whether the Queen was involved in it has never been established.

By now Mary's story was in a rapid downward spiral. In May Bothwell both divorced his wife and married the Queen. Darnley may have been despised, but this precipitate marriage was too much for most Scottish people. They rose up against the royal pair, whose meagre forces were routed in a skirmish at Carberry Hill near Dunbar. Bothwell escaped, leaving his bride to be imprisoned in the island castle of Loch Leven, north of Glasgow, and on 24 July, she was forced to abdicate in favour of her infant son, James VI. The following year (1568) she escaped, rallying some forces to her side, but was defeated once again at Langside near Glasgow. After that she fled to England and spent nearly 20 lonely years as the prisoner of her cousin, Queen Elizabeth, finally facing execution in 1587.

The grit of the Glaswegians

Scotland's two major cities – Glasgow and Edinburgh, lying within 40 miles of each other on the country's narrow central neck – present a series of contrasts: Edinburgh with its Georgian architecture, Glasgow with its Victorian buildings; Edinburgh facing east, Glasgow west; Edinburgh largely professional, Glasgow industrial; Edinburgh people traditionally refined, Glaswegians brash. The rivalry between the two cities is intense. In the 1980s Glasgow ran a publicity campaign in which the slogan 'Glasgow – miles better' appeared on the sides of London buses and elsewhere. Better than what? Than Edinburgh was the implication.

The truth is that Glasgow is a place of huge vitality that in the last few decades has tackled the problems of

Highland fling (below). Scottish country dances such as the 'Gay Gordons', 'Eightsome Reel' and 'Dashing White Sergeant' are hugely popular at parties and gatherings, not just in Scotland, but also among the 'Sassenachs' (Saxons) south of the border.

The sporran hanging from his belt, plaid hanging down his back, and dirk (dagger) poking from his stockings – these are among the accoutrements of the full-dress Highland piper or drummer of today (right). Things were rather simpler for his ancestors. They made do with the breacan-feile, *or belted plaid, which was a long tartan blanket. They wrapped one end around their waists and hung the rest over their shoulders, the whole precarious assembly held in place by a pin or brooch. This was hardly fighting gear, so before battles they would sometimes cast the plaid aside and fight near naked. At night they could use the plaid to sleep in.*

It was the Romans who introduced the bagpipes to Britain (far right). The instrument is by no means unique to Scotland, and traces of early versions of it have been found in Egypt, Greece and Persia. But of course, the Scots have made it especially their own. The bagpipes work like miniature organs. The piper blows into a bag which he squeezes with his arm to produce the characteristic drone and melodies.

Highland Games are summer occasions, popular with locals and tourists alike. Events include relatively straightforward affairs, such as a tug of war and foot races, as well as others which are more specialised: putting the stone, throwing the hammer and tossing the caber (right). The best-known of the Games is the Braemar Gathering, in the eastern Highlands, said to have been started by an 11th-century Scottish king who chose his messengers from the fleetest of foot in the races. Later, Queen Victoria was a devotee, and the Royal Family still arrive in force from nearby Balmoral, the male members suitably kilted.

industrial decline more successfully than almost any other comparable British city – and in the process has come up with a remarkable cultural renaissance. Not so long ago contemporary Glasgow was known chiefly for urban decay, appalling slums in areas such as the Gorbals and unusually high levels of violent crime.

No longer. Since the 1960s slums have been cleared and city-centre buildings cleaned. George Square at the heart of Glasgow, overlooked by the ornate Victorian City Chambers, buzzes with activity, while streets such as the nearby pedestrian-only Buchanan Street, are lined with smart shops. Since 1975 the Theatre Royal has been home to the highly respected Scottish National Opera. There are many new arts centres and Glasgow's Mayfest is beginning to rival the Edinburgh Festival. In 1983 the city's crowning cultural glory, the Burrell Collection, was opened – a superb collection of art and antiquities bequeathed by the shipowner Sir William Burrell. A final tribute to Glasgow's remarkable regeneration came when it was chosen in preference to Bath, Cambridge and, above all, Edinburgh as European City of Culture for 1990.

the huge mountain block of the Cairngorms dominates the uplands, with nine peaks rising to over 4000 ft. There are few lochs in this part of the Highlands but, as if to make up for it, two great rivers, the Spey and Dee, have gouged out broad valleys. Running north along the west side of the Cairngorm massif is Scotland's chief whisky-producing region, Speyside. It also has Aviemore, a skiing centre in winter. Deeside runs roughly east, with the Royal Family's Balmoral Castle as its most famous landmark. The North Sea oil-boom city of Aberdeen lies at its mouth, on the edge of a broad coastal region of rolling farmlands stretching to the north and east.

The west coast is quite different. Here, mountains are generally lower and more spread out, descending to the sea in a confusion of islands, islets, freshwater lochs and fjord-like sea lochs. Ferries link Oban on the shores of the Firth of Lorn in the south-west with islands such as Mull and Colonsay, and beyond them to the southern end of the Outer Hebrides. In the Inner Hebrides, the tiny island of Iona off Mull is one of the most ancient seats of Christianity in Scotland, the princely Irish missionary St Columba founding a monastery there in AD 563. Even tinier is Staffa to the north, largely composed of strikingly symmetrical basalt columns and famous for the 65-foot-high sea cavern, Fingal's Cave, which inspired the composer Mendelssohn to write his *Hebrides Overture*.

Back on the mainland running north-east from Fort William, another fault line cuts its way through the Highlands: the Great Glen, marked by a series of long, narrow lochs. At its northern end, lying at the mouth of Loch Ness is Inverness, a growing commercial and

Tossing the caber (a tall pine log) requires considerable skill as well as enormous beefy strength. The contestant must hurl the caber into the air so that it flips right over and lands with the end the thrower was holding pointing away from him. The key is to get the caber properly balanced before tossing it.

The glories of the Highlands

A glance at a map reveals the Highland line – a fault in the Earth's surface – slicing diagonally across Scotland from Helensburgh on the Clyde to Stonehaven on the east coast. To the south lie the northern stretches of the Lowlands, with the industrial city of Dundee on the Firth of Tay and historic places such as Stirling, Perth and the university city of St Andrews (famous also for the Royal and Ancient Golf Club, one of the ruling bodies of world golf) on the coast of the Fife peninsula. North of the line, meanwhile, rise the mountains and heather-clad moors of the Highlands, one of Europe's last wilderness regions.

When people think of Scotland they tend to think of the Highlands – to the frequent irritation of Lowlanders. It is certainly an awe-inspiring landscape, covering one-sixth of the area of Britain. North of the Highland line, shopping centre for the Highlands. People have reported sightings of the loch's famous monster since St Columba's time, and in modern times there have been several scientific investigations to try to find out what could lie behind the stories, but no one has yet come up with an explanation. At the south-western end of the Great Glen the solitary mass of Britain's highest peak, Ben Nevis (4406 feet), overlooks the old garrison town of Fort William.

It is a landscape of unparalleled splendour, but once again reminders of a bloody past abound. Culloden, east of Inverness, was the site of Bonnie Prince Charlie's final defeat in April 1746. Glencoe, south of Ben Nevis, was the scene of the treacherous massacre in 1692 of 38 members of the Macdonald clan (including two women and two children) by soldiers acting under government orders and led by a member of the widely hated Campbell clan.

Not that the Highland clansmen needed the interference of outsiders to provoke violence among them. Much mythology has grown up around the clans of the Highlands. For one of the best-loved of modern clan chiefs, Dame Flora McLeod, who died aged 98 in 1976, the clan family was 'beyond and outside divisions between nations, countries and continents ... it takes no note of age or rank or wealth, success or failure ... Clanship embraces them all.' And yet the truth about the clans of old, at least, seems to be less benign. Originally groups bound together by loose ties of kinship, they came increasingly under the sway of autocratic chieftains whose word was law for their

devoted followers. Highland society, separated from the increasingly anglicised Lowlands by barriers of geography, culture and language (until the 18th century most Highlanders spoke Gaelic), was frequently riven by petty rivalry between the chieftains, leading to sporadic inter-clan warfare.

The Western Isles stretch out along the Atlantic rim of the Hebrides. These lovely islands are shaped rather like a highly fragmented tadpole. In the north the larger island of Harris and Lewis (famous for its handwoven tweed) forms the head and body of the tadpole, while the chain of smaller islands to the south, from North Uist at the top to the tiny dot of Berneray at the bottom, forms its tail. Even more than along the west coast of the mainland, the landscape here is an enchanting jumble of sea, loch, low moor and bog.

The Western Isles are also one of the last strongholds of the Gaelic language. For a long time this seemed destined to a slow, dwindling death. In fact, it is now making a modest comeback. Back on the mainland, the old counties of Caithness and Sutherland in the far north are a bleak wilderness of bog and mountains, and are the most sparsely populated area in the British Isles. Red sandstone cliffs rise sheer for 850 feet from the Atlantic on Cape Wrath, the mainland's far north-western tip. Off Duncansby Head, the north-eastern tip a few miles from John O'Groats, the Duncansby Stacks have been chiselled to fine points by wind and waves. Here the tides run swift through the Pentland Firth, which separates the mainland from the islands of Orkney to the north.

Like grouse shooting and deer stalking, salmon fishing tends to be a sport for well-off outsiders who make regular summer pilgrimages to Scotland from their city jobs. Fishing rights on famous salmon rivers such as the Spey and Tay are jealously guarded by their owners, though local poachers take delight in eluding their restrictions. The fishermen use large artificial flies, skilfully concocted from feathers and tinsel, to lure the salmon.

Ireland

The easy-going pace of Irish life is legendary. In the 'Emerald Isle'
no amount of economic or social woes are allowed to stand in the
way of a whole-hearted enjoyment of the pleasures of living ...
whether these lie in the excitement of the race track, the harmonies
of 'singing' pubs or the gentle art of passing the time of day.
The scenery is magnificent, ranging from the windswept glories of
the West Coast to the subtler beauties of the fertile central plain.

The charm of Clifden, the 'capital of Connemara', owes a lot to its site above an inlet of the Atlantic. The Twelve Pins provide a grand backdrop to the town against the eastern sky.

Previous page:
The Viking blood in this fisherman from the island of Inishbofin off Connemara on the West Coast stands out clearly. The name Inishbofin comes from the Gaelic for 'island of the white cow', after the white cow belonging to a witch who, legend has it, kept the island hidden in mist until two fishermen stumbled on it and broke the spell by lighting a fire on the shore.

Two County Mayo fishermen take it easy after a day at sea. The Atlantic waters off Mayo are rich in fish, and local fishermen still make a satisfactory living from the harvest of the sea. Inland, meanwhile, the county's streams, rivers and loughs offer some of the best freshwater fishing in Ireland.

Isle of Saints and Scholars

Few nations in western Europe have suffered more than the Irish. Their country was invaded in the late 8th century by Vikings from Scandinavia and in the 12th century by Normans from Wales and England; it was ruthlessly subjugated in the 17th century by Oliver Cromwell and his Ironsides; and it suffered the Great Famine of the 1840s, in which one million people died. Even after the Republic of Ireland had finally won its freedom from Britain in the early 20th century, the north of the island was still bedevilled by the continuing and bloody strife between Catholic and Protestant men of violence.

And yet, if the Irish have suffered more than most over the centuries, they have also shown an extraordinary resilience of spirit. Despite pressing contemporary social and economic problems as well as the memories of past sufferings, they remain among the most warm-hearted, friendly and vivacious of nations. Their traditional popular culture, especially in the field of music, is one of the most vital in Europe, while from the very earliest times they have shown outstanding gifts in the fields of learning and literature. The Celtic Ireland of the 3rd to 8th centuries was famed as the 'Isle of Saints and Scholars'. It was a beacon of learning, shining from the Atlantic fringes of a Europe engulfed in the Dark Ages. Irish monasteries such as Clonmacnoise west of Dublin and St Enda's on the remote Aran Islands off the West Coast kept alive traditions of scholarship inherited from Greece and Rome, and produced marvels such as the 9th-century illuminated manuscript, the *Book of Kells,* now kept at Trinity College, Dublin.

In more recent centuries the Irish have produced a seemingly endless list of major writers: playwrights from William Congreve, Richard Brinsley Sheridan, Oscar Wilde and George Bernard Shaw to J.M. Synge, Sean O'Casey, Brendan Behan and Samuel Beckett; satirists such as Jonathan Swift (author of *Gulliver's Travels*); political writers such as Edmund Burke; poets such as W.B. Yeats; novelists such as James Joyce and Flann O'Brien; and even the author of *Dracula,* Bram Stoker. It is a tradition that continues with a clutch of highly regarded contemporary writers including the poet Seamus Heaney and the novelist Brian Moore.

Darkness and light mingle strangely in Ireland, now as they always have done – on the one hand, Ireland is a land of creative vitality and sophistication, on the other it is one of the poorer countries of western Europe. It

Aran Island knitwear and garments made from the coarse, hard-wearing, locally woven cloth have become popular with outsiders in recent years – providing a profitable cottage industry for many islanders. Tourism is also important; visitors arriving by mail boat have to make the last lap of the journey to the rocky shore in traditional curraghs – long, narrow boats made of tarred canvas stretched over a wooden framework.

At 3127 ft, Brandon Mountain is Ireland's second-highest peak. With its rugged mountains and wave-lashed coves, County Kerry is one of the most popular counties in Ireland.

has a per capita income less than half that of France. Its economy relies substantially on tourists, drawn above all by the mountain splendours of the rugged West Coast, and on the agricultural production of the fertile central plain. There is relatively little industry and a consequent shortage of jobs. The last few decades have seen an upturn in emigration (one of Ireland's blights since the 18th century), with thousands of young people, including many of the brightest and best-qualified, leaving the country each year for a brighter future in America and Britain.

At the same time the Roman Catholic Church has kept Irish society in an exceptionally tight grip. Ireland is easily the most Catholic country in western Europe. A recent survey of a number of countries showed that around 65 per cent of people in the Republic attend at least one church service a week – only Protestant Northern Ireland came anywhere near, with around 55 per cent. In recent years the Church has quite openly used its influence against reforming the laws on abortion and divorce. Abortion is illegal in the Republic, and Government proposals to legalise divorce

The bright pink and yellow blooms of wild flowers stand out against the grey of the rocky Atlantic coastline. Among the delights of the wilder parts of Ireland are the bright splashes of colour where flowers like these can flourish in a landscape still largely untouched by modern farming methods. The pattern is continued inland, where huge areas of peat bog – covering one-seventh of the Republic – continue to survive and provide the chief indigenous source of fuel.

Connemara's dappled grey ponies are famed for their hardiness, good nature and intelligence – making them ideal for children and inexperienced trekkers. Each year, on the third Thursday in August, they are judged and sold to buyers from all over the world at the Connemara Pony Show, one of the big events at Clifden, the region's principal town.

were voted down in a referendum in 1986.

But signs of change are there. In the last few years, for example, there have been new stirrings of economic activity in parts of the country. While, on the one hand, a government determined to reduce its huge international debt has cut back on social spending (with devastating results in the poorer areas of Dublin), cities such as Limerick and Galway on the West Coast have experienced remarkable growth, drawing increasing investment from multinational computer and high-tech businesses. Galway, in particular, claims to be one of the fastest-growing cities in Europe.

Signs of social change have also emerged. With 50 per cent of its population aged under 28, Ireland is an overwhelmingly young country, and more and more young people are questioning age-old attitudes on issues such as the role of women and the place of the Church. In 1990 the 46-year-old barrister and Harvard-trained academic lawyer Mary Robinson surprised many observers by winning the presidential election after a campaign fought on a firmly secular and modernising platform. Admittedly, the President's role is largely ceremonial, but her victory in a traditionally male-dominated society seemed to indicate new outlooks. As she herself put it: 'The hand that rocked the cradle has rocked the system.'

Dublin's fair city

Dublin has always elicited love-hate reactions from those living or born there. 'How sick, sick, sick I am of Dublin!' complained James Joyce. 'It is the city of failure, of rancour and unhappiness. I long to be out of it.' George Bernard Shaw was even more dismissive: 'My sentimental regard for Ireland does not include the capital.' The truth is that Dublin, like Ireland as a whole, is a place of contradictions and contrasts, infuriating and charming at the same time. Poverty rubs shoulders with affluence in its streets, shabbiness with a predominantly Georgian elegance. But always the majority of Dubliners manage to live life with a splendid zest, singing in their pubs, gambling ferociously at the dog tracks in the east of the city and, at the weekends, turning out in force for horse races at the Curragh on the plains of County Kildare to the south-west.

The River Liffey divides the city into two halves – the North Side and the South Side. During the 1960s and '70s large parts of the city were redeveloped, with – to the horror of many – a number of Georgian terraces and tenements bulldozed to make way for largely nondescript modern buildings. Even so, plenty of Georgian elegance survives, even on the North Side. In

Wild Atlantic winds howl across the West Coast, and the thatched roofs of traditional cottages have to be pegged down to keep them safe. In recent decades many of these cottages have been bought as holiday homes by people from Britain and Northern Europe – and some have settled in them for good, fleeing the hustle of modern urban life and relishing the famously easy pace of Irish life.

the east the great, domed Custom House dominates a bend in the Liffey and in the west rise the Four Courts, housing the High Court of Justice of Ireland – both the work of one of the most talented of Dublin's Georgian architects, James Gandon.

In the middle of the 18th century, fashion moved from the North Side to the South Side where it has stayed ever since. Westmoreland Street running south from O'Connell Bridge is dominated by the rough-hewn, classical front of Trinity College, Dublin, originally founded in 1592 by Elizabeth I, and long the most important university college in Ireland. Burke, Swift, Bram Stoker, Synge and Beckett were all educated here. To the south again, shoppers throng the pedestrians-only Grafton Street which has Dublin's two great department stores, Switzers and Brown Thomas. Tucked among the shops is one of the Bewley's Oriental Cafés, wonderful havens of wood-panelling and marble-topped tables, where clients, including politicians, business people or figures from the arts

Thatched roofs need constant maintenance. Traditional crafts and arts survive well in Ireland and, despite the increasing importance of tourism, they keep an authentic feel – for Irish people quite simply love their old customs and patterns of life. In folk music especially, they are without equal in western Europe – each region has its own distinctive style, the range of instruments including the fiddle, the tin whistle and even bones and spoons.

A shearer holds the head of a sheep firmly between his knees while he clips off the precious crop of wool. Ireland's wool products include the knitwear of the Aran Islands and the tweeds of Connemara and Donegal. Farther east, the manufacture of linen, made from the fibres of the flax plant, remains an important industry, especially in rural Ulster. Crisp Irish linen tablecloths, napkins and sheets are prized throughout the world.

world, meet friends for a coffee or simply sit and read the papers.

St Stephen's Green opens out at the foot of Grafton Street. Running off it is Kildare Street with Leinster House, built in the 18th century for the 1st Duke of Leinster and now home of the Irish Parliament (Dail Eireann). A few blocks to the east is one of the finest of Dublin's Georgian squares, Merrion Square, where Yeats lived, as did Oscar Wilde's parents, the eye surgeon Sir William Wilde and his poet wife Speranza. Over to the west are the surviving fragments of medieval Dublin – the Castle, partly Norman and for centuries the seat of British administration in Ireland, and the two Church of Ireland (Anglican) cathedrals, St Patrick's and Christchurch. Beyond these are the narrow, grimy streets

of The Liberties, once a French Huguenot area, which is now dominated by the chimneys of the Guinness brewery. Across the Liffey from the brewery lies Phoenix Park, which is the largest urban park in Europe.

Anglo-Irish splendour

As Dublin's architecture indicates, the 18th century was in many ways one of the city's most splendid eras. In the previous century, Cromwell had followed his bloody conquest of Ireland by rewarding numbers of his soldiers (all Protestants, of course) with estates confiscated from their former Catholic owners. The

Anglo-Irish gentry who are mostly descended from these settlers hold an uneasy place in Irish history – sometimes hated as often oppressive landlords, yet also producing some of the greatest of Irish patriots, including the 19th-century campaigner for Home Rule, Charles Stewart Parnell, as well as other figures such as the poet Yeats. They certainly proved a vigorous and talented race. In the 18th century Dublin was one of the finest cities in Europe. Lashed by the unsparing and most irreverent pen of Swift, Dean of St Patrick's Cathedral from 1713 to 1745, the Anglo-Irish built the capital's Georgian glories, as well as Ireland's many superb country houses, such as Westport House in County Mayo on the West Coast, Bantry House in the south and Powerscourt just south of Dublin. Commerce and the

A herd of cows makes its way down a country lane, while in the background strips of sandy beach shelter between lonely, green headlands. The shamrock green of the Irish countryside is the product of its mild, humid and ever-changing climate. Warm fronts sweep in from the Atlantic at any time of the year, drenching the land beneath sheets of low cloud. Then a cold front will arrive, bringing bright skies and drifting showers that endow the landscape with a sparkling brilliance of colour.

arts flourished – Handel's *Messiah* was first performed in Dublin in 1742 – and by the end of the century the Dublin parliament (dominated by the fiery orator Henry Grattan) had secured effective Home Rule for Ireland.

However, it was very much Ireland for the Protestant Anglo-Irish. From 1692 a savage Penal Code came into force which systematically discriminated against the native Catholic Irish. Catholics were not allowed to vote in General Elections or to stand for Parliament; they were forbidden to educate their children in their faith; and rack-renting Protestant landlords kept their peasantry in the direst poverty.

High Kings of Ireland who presided over a hundred or so smaller kingdoms grouped into the provinces of Leinster, Munster, Connaught and Ulster. Rising from Dundalk Bay on the borders with Northern Ireland are the rounded, heather-clad mountains of the small Cooley peninsula – *Cuailgne* in Gaelic – where many of the events of the Celtic epic, the *Táin Bó Cuailgne* (*Cattle Raid of Cooley*), took place. This is a splendidly rumbustious account of how the hero Cúchulainn single-handedly defended the tribes of Ulster from the armies and wiles of Queen Maeve of Connaught in the west, determined to carry off the prodigious Brown Bull of Cooley. Drogheda to the south brings back grimmer

The beauties of the east

Dublin lies about halfway down Ireland's east coast, more or less on a level with Liverpool in England. To its north extend the plains of Meath and Louth, rich in historical associations. Tara in Meath was the seat of the

Hydrangeas love a damp climate and so find a perfect environment in Ireland. They provide yet another bold splash of colour in cottage gardens and often establish themselves in the wild, sheltering under dry-stone walls or high banks of earth. They are generally a purplish-pink but also take on a brilliant azure blue when growing in the shaly soil that covers many parts of Ireland.

Centuries of antagonism may lie between the Irish and the English, but they share one thing – a love of gardening. Especially in the more domesticated lands of central and south-eastern Ireland, cottage gardens present an almost garish abundance of colour, while green creepers clamber up the cottage walls to the thatched eaves.

memories – in September 1649 Cromwell's Ironsides massacred its Royalist garrison of 2000, as well as many clergy and townspeople.

South of Dublin rise the wild Wicklow Mountains where the unruly, outlaw O'Toole and O'Byrne clans held out for centuries. In places they slope right down to the sea, where the coastline is characterised by rocky inlets, sandy beaches and busy fishing villages. Apart from the Wicklow Way, there are few footpaths marked out in the mountains. The mountains give way to the more domesticated lushness of Ireland's south-eastern corner. The port city of Wexford is one of the Republic's industrial centres – it also holds an opera festival each October, an important event in the international operatic calendar. Around the corner from Wexford, on the south coast, Waterford is famous for hand-cut crystal glass – its glass factory is the largest of its kind in the world. Both these coastal cities, like many in Ireland (also including Dublin, Cork and Limerick), were first settled by Viking invaders, who stayed and intermarried with the native Irish. Inland, meanwhile, mountain ranges descend gradually to the central plain, leaving broad and fertile valleys between them, such as the dairy-farming area of the Golden Vale striking towards the West Coast through Counties Tipperary and Limerick. The area also has many

Widely different rhythms of life somehow manage to survive and co-exist in Ireland: on the one hand, the high-tech marvels of booming West Coast cities such as Limerick and Galway; on the other, an age-old peasant culture where homes are primitive – to modern eyes at least – and life can be harsh. But always there is that characteristic Irish love of colour, seen in the bold reds and blues of the women's traditional costumes.

remains of Bronze Age settlements and burial sites. To the south-west of Dublin is County Kildare, home of the Curragh racecourse where the five Irish classic races – including the Irish Derby – are run. Racing stables and stud farms – including Ireland's National Stud, where some of the world's top racehorses have been bred – are clustered around the Curragh, where the local turf is ideal for training racehorses.

The south-eastern corner was the starting point of the Norman invasion of Ireland – and remains one of the most anglicised parts of the Republic. The leading figure in this episode was the Welsh Norman knight and adventurer Richard FitzGilbert, long in pedigree but short in purse, more commonly known as Strongbow. The Normans were brought to Ireland, like the Greeks to Troy, because of trouble over a woman. Dermot MacMurrough, King of Leinster, fell in love with Dervorgilla, wife of Tiernan O'Rourke, Prince of Breifne, and abducted her. The outraged husband eventually defeated him in battle, deposed him and seized back his wife. Dermot, with neither kingdom nor

Dervorgilla to his name crossed the sea to England in 1166, to plead for help in regaining his throne. Small Norman contingents landed in 1167 and 1169; finally in August 1170 Strongbow himself arrived with 1000 men off Waterford, which was being held by Dermot's enemies. They stormed the city after a siege of three days, and a grateful Dermot gave Strongbow his only daughter and heir, Eva, in marriage. Later that year Strongbow took Dublin.

When Dermot died in May 1171 Strongbow found himself lord of Leinster – a turn of events that worried Henry II of England. In October that year, he too sailed for Ireland determined to assert his authority not only over Strongbow but over the island as a whole – an enterprise for which he later received papal blessing. At a meeting of the Irish kings and bishops at Cashel in County Tipperary, Henry proclaimed himself feudal overlord of Ireland. Thus began the turbulent relationship between the two lands.

The Norman overlordship of Ireland was never more than a tenuous affair. The area centred on Dublin under

Delicious pastel colours prevail in this small town street, as in so many across Ireland. The hour is early and the street empty, but already the greengrocer has his awning up and vegetables on display. Ireland is still a strongly agricultural country, and life moves to the hours and rhythms of the seasons.

the control of the English crown – the Pale as it came to be known, with those living in the wild lands beyond deemed to be 'beyond the pale' – never included more than a relatively small portion of Ireland. The Normans were constantly harrassed by local lords, until by the end of the Middle Ages the Pale was reduced to a narrow strip around Dublin. However, there are many signs of the Norman occupation. The area is scattered with the remains of their castles, such as those at Carlow, Wicklow and Enniscorthy, and many more lie in ruins and overgrown. There is also a Norman lighthouse at Hook Head.

Cork and the west

The Republic's second city, Cork, lies west along the coast from Waterford. It is a heady, invigorating place, centred on a large island in the River Lee. What it lacks in fine architecture, it makes up for with charm – its quays busy with markets and small shipping (dealing in the dairy products of the farming areas inland). On St Patrick's Street and Grand Parade fashion boutiques jostle in happy confusion with small traditional haberdashers and ironmongers; elsewhere the narrow lanes bustle as the hugely friendly Corkonians go about

No wonder foreign visitors love Ireland. It may be one of western Europe's poorer countries, but the care and devotion lavished on the finer things of life – so that even a barber's shop front is a minor work of art – give it an irresistible appeal.

Supermarkets may have taken over in the big cities, but in rural Ireland the small, family-owned shop still reigns supreme. These are communities where everyone knows everyone else, and in some parts of the remote West the ancient Gaelic language is still the mother tongue of most people.

their daily business. Tourism, industry and the port bring Cork commercial prosperity, and it is also an important cultural centre, with one of the colleges of the federal National University of Ireland, an opera house and the modern Triskel Arts Centre. In September and October Cork also hosts an international jazz festival and a film festival.

A few miles north-west of Cork rise the medieval walls of Blarney Castle, where for a hundred years or more tourists have been prepared to go through perilous contortions hanging backwards over the battlements to kiss the famous Blarney Stone, which is said to grant them the all-important gifts of eloquence and flattery. The story thought to lie behind this legend concerns Dermot McCarthy, lord of Blarney and King of Munster in the time of Elizabeth I of England. Although theoretically loyal to the Queen, Dermot rarely carried out any of her instructions. When royal envoys were sent to him he simply wined, feasted and entertained them, and then sent them back home again. Finally in a fit of exasperation, Elizabeth is said to have cried out: 'Blarney, Blarney, what he says he does not mean. It is the usual Blarney.'

Ireland's south-west corner, with the three deep inlets of Bantry Bay, Kenmare River and Dingle Bay, has some of the country's most spectacular scenery. Cliffs plunge dizzyingly at Mizen Head in the south, where gusting winds whip the spray of thundering Atlantic rollers miles inland, while at night the beam of the lighthouse winks from Fastnet Rock far out to sea. Farther north the Cahir Mountains climb from Bantry Bay, and beyond them is the Ivereagh peninsula, where the range known as MacGillycuddy's Reeks rises to Ireland's highest peak, Carrantuohill (3414 feet). A circuit of the Ivereagh peninsula can be made along the Ring of Kerry, which starts in Killarney and takes in

both mountains and coast road. On the Dingle peninsula, the ruins of castles and monasteries stand on lonely headlands, together with early Christian remains, including 1000-year-old beehive huts where people lived, while all around moors are studded with the yellow of gorse and the rich red of wild fuchsias. The Gulf Stream gives this part of the coast a very mild climate, and many Mediterranean plants can be seen in the several gardens open to the public. Small farming communities include surviving *Gaeltacht* (Irish-speaking) areas, though other tongues are also heard. During the 1960s many young Scandinavians, Germans and other North Europeans – known to the locals as 'blow-ins' – settled here to escape the rigours of modern life.

The West Coast continues the pattern of wild scenery – most of it lying within the province of Connaught bounded to the east by the River Shannon. The Aran Islands rise from Galway Bay, while climbing from its southern shore is the strange, barren landscape of the Burren, a series of huge, windswept limestone shelves, covering nearly 200 square miles and reaching 1134 feet at Slieve Elva in the east. Galway City near the head of the bay is a pocket of commerce and prosperity. As well as having a booming high-tech industry, it is an important centre for Irish culture and music, holding a number of annual festivals. In the Middle Ages the city was an outpost of Norman power and influence, whose 14 families ('the 14 tribes of Galway') held out against the fierce onslaughts of the local Irish clans, above all the O'Flaherties. One gateway held the hopeful inscription: 'From the fury of the O'Flaherties, good Lord deliver us.'

The sparsely populated wilds of Connemara rise from Galway Bay's northern shores, a glorious region of lakes, moors and peat bogs, dominated by the peaks known as the Twelve Bens and the Maumturk

The annual summer horse fair is a big occasion for many country towns in western and central Ireland – an opportunity for friends and relatives to meet as well as to conduct business. The biggest and most famous fair is the one at Ballinasloe on the borders of Counties Galway and Roscommon. It lasts for eight days at the beginning of October and draws horse dealers from England as well as from all over Ireland.

Bartering is an essential part of the ritual at the fairs. Both these men undoubtedly know exactly how much the horse they are haggling over is worth, but feel that the sale will not have been properly concluded unless each has got the other to move on his price.

Mountains. Atlantic waves fall on miles of spotless, white-sand beaches, while offshore lie numerous small islands. Road signs here are all in Gaelic and in some areas a few of the older people still speak English with some difficulty. The land here is poor, and the people have always struggled to make a living from fishing and turf-cutting. The bogs are also a rich source of information about the past, as everything from pollen grains to tombs is preserved in them.

The Connemara mountains are also home to the Connemara pony, a breed that dates back to the Middle Ages. It probably developed as a result of crossing ancient native Celtic ponies with Arab-type horses imported from north-west Spain. The rugged environment has produced a pony that is very strong and hardy, yet it is also good natured and is a popular riding pony. Pony fairs are a regular and colourful event in the area.

County Mayo to the north offers some of Ireland's best fishing, and also has Knock, where the Virgin accompanied by St Joseph and St John is said to have appeared to some local people in 1879 – it is now a centre of pilgrimage, visited by Pope John Paul II in 1979, and is served by its own airport. The coastline here is ragged and dramatic, and it is sometimes completely obliterated by the thick mists that roll in off the Atlantic.

The mountains and lakes of County Sligo to the east are famous as Yeats country, where the poet and his painter brother Jack spent much of their childhood. Lough Gill east of Sligo City has Yeats's 'Lake Isle of Inisfree' – the poet himself is buried at Drumcliff, at the foot of Benbulbin, to the north. Numerous prehistoric tombs, ring-forts and *crannogs* (lake dwellings) would

suggest that the region was heavily populated in the past. County Leitrim was once barely accessible, and was the stronghold of the powerful O'Rourke family until it was settled by planters in the 17th century. The River Shannon, a mecca for salmon and trout fishermen, runs through it.

The years of suffering

With the exception of places such as Galway, Connaught with County Clare to its south has traditionally been one of Ireland's poorest regions. It was also the scene of some of the worst sufferings at the hands of Cromwell in the 17th century and during the Great Famine 200 years later.

Cromwell arrived in Ireland in August 1649, a few months after the execution of Charles I, determined to quell the last major bastion of royalist resistance. In just under a year's campaigning, he and his Ironsides swept across the island from Drogheda in the north-east to

The 19th-century nationalist leader Daniel O'Connell stares down from his plinth on Dublin's O'Connell Street. In the foreground a Guinness lorry moves in to deliver a cargo of precious black stout to a pub. Arthur Guinness opened his brewery in 1759, and it has never looked back. The present brewery spreads over 64 acres of south-western Dublin, and the company can claim to be the biggest exporter of stout in the world.

Cork in the south-west, leaving thousands dead behind them. Cromwell next embarked on an even more ruthless campaign of transplantation, aimed at breaking Catholic Ireland for ever. According to this, the bulk of the Catholic population above the rank of the poorest labourers was to be shifted bodily, and on pain of death, to the west of the Shannon – to 'Hell or Connaught' in a phrase that became famous. It was a cruel business in which entire families were uprooted from communities in which they had lived for generations, many dying during the journey west.

The sufferings of the Great Famine were even worse. For generations Irish peasants had subsisted almost exclusively on potatoes. In a succession of crops from 1845 onwards, these fell prey to blight – a fungal disease that rotted the tubers in the ground or in store. The results were appalling. In 1847 alone, 250,000 people died from starvation and an epidemic of typhoid, while a further 3 million were kept alive only by public funds. Many landlords sacrificed fortunes trying to save their tenants; others simply evicted them.

Before the Famine, Ireland had supported a population of more than 8 million people – the island's present population (including North and South) is just over 5 million. By the end of a decade it had lost 2 million people, of whom roughly a million died. The rest emigrated, mostly to North America and Australia. Thus began the drain on the Irish population which has continued to a greater or lesser extent to this day, with the result, for example, that New York now has the largest Irish population of any city in the world. In the Republic the tale of emigration is told by the ruined and deserted hamlets, abandoned fields and forgotten peat diggings that lie scattered throughout western Ireland.

High winds in Donegal

The ancient province of Ulster begins on the West Coast with Donegal – though the county's Catholic majority meant that Ulster's Protestant leaders agreed to surrender it to the Republic when Ireland was partitioned in 1921. Of all the West Coast's wild

March 17 is St Patrick's Day. The feast of Ireland's patron saint is celebrated with equal gusto in Ireland and among the Irish communities abroad, especially America. Tartans and uilleann *(elbow) pipes – a reminder of the Irish people's Celtic kinship with the Scots – are very much the order of the day, as people parade through the streets and attend special masses.*

Even in cities as sophisticated as Dublin and Cork, the horse-drawn cart still holds its place, making sure that the pace of life never gets too hectic.

regions this is perhaps the wildest. It has the highest cliffs in Europe where the Slieve League mountain plummets 1800 feet to the Atlantic, and Malin Head, at the northerly end of the Inishowen peninsula, is the most northerly point in Ireland. Winds howl across rocky headlands and over lonely inland glens and peat bogs. It also has the largest number of Gaelic-speakers of any Irish region. It was the home of St Columba, who founded the monastery at Kells, and who was eventually banished and went on to found the community on Iona, off the west coast of Scotland.

The River Swilly, which flows through northern Donegal, is said to get its name from Suileach, a monster killed by St Columba. As the saint passed the pool where Suileach lived, it rushed out at him, but he cut it in half with his sword, and when both halves attacked him, he cut it into small pieces and then washed his sword in the Swilly, saying that the water would wash away anger, as it had washed away the monster's blood.

Lough Swilly brings back memories of the engaging revolutionary Wolfe Tone. A barrister by training (like so many Irish nationalist leaders) with a delightfully

high-spirited nature, he helped to found the Society of United Irishmen which sought to bring together Protestant and Catholic Irishmen of good will. This brought him into trouble with the authorities, and he fled first to America and then to revolutionary France whose ideals had inspired him. He and a small French fleet bringing support for a nationalist rebellion in 1798 were captured off Lough Swilly in September that year. Tone was sentenced to death but he preferred to use a pocket knife to cut his own throat rather than face execution – he eventually died after a week of agony.

Northern glories

Northern Ireland is a troubled land today, but it too has an abundance of fine scenery. In the west the lonely moorland farming country of Fermanagh and Tyrone rises to the Sperrin Mountains – more gentle hills than mountains and dotted with Stone-Age standing stones – that overlook Londonderry. Londonderry, known as Derry to the Catholics in Ulster, is Northern Ireland's second-largest city. It was built by a group of City of London companies, who were granted land in return for colonising, or 'planting', the area – thus the addition to its name. The city walls are a mile in circumference and are still intact. Londonderry stands on the River Foyle a few miles in from the Atlantic coast to the north. Many people set out for the New World from here during the 19th century, and at the Ulster-American Folk Park there are authentic reconstructions of the type of old Ulster buildings that the emigrants left behind, and of the log cabins that they built in the New World. There is also a replica of a 19th-century sailing ship similar to the *Union*, in which emigrants travelled to America.

Over to the east the emerald-green glens of the Antrim Mountains fall steeply to the sea, while on the north coast is the spectacular complex of basaltic columns known as the Giant's Causeway. According to legend, the causeway was built by the giant, Finn MacCool, so that he could step across the sea from Ireland to Scotland. The real-life cause, however, is that

Two old-timers swap views about the state of the world in a Dublin pub. The spoken word is relished in Ireland – conversation is an art form, whether in the pub, the office or the drawing room, and turns of phrase are often ingenious, owing much to memories of Gaelic. If an Irish person tells you he is 'as full as a trout', he means that he is bursting with food; if he says of someone that he is 'as fat in the forehead as a hen', he means that the person is particularly dense and unintelligent.

Music is important for even the youngest Irish people. Musicians regularly gather for pub 'sessions' when they spend evenings improvising traditional airs or more modern melodies. At weekends céilí bands perform for village dances, where country and western numbers imported from America mingle a little strangely with rebel ballads such as The Croppy Boy *and sad love songs.*

Along with the clover leaf, the harp is one of Ireland's national emblems. In Celtic times, bards accompanying themselves on harps would entertain the courts of Irish kings. Some kings, notably the great 11th-century High King Brian Boru, were harpists in their own right. Since those days, however, the harp has fallen out of favour as a popular instrument, and the traditions of the bards have died.

the pillars were formed by cooling and contracting volcanic rock. These fantastic structures have been given evocative names such as the Wishing Chair, the Honeycomb, the Giant's Loom and the Harp. Rathlin Island, off the north Antrim coast, is said to have been dropped into the sea by Finn MacCool's mother on her way to Scotland. Flint instruments have been found there that could be as much as 6000 years old. It is said to be the first place in Ireland to be raided by the Vikings in the 8th century, and legend has it that the King of Norway was killed in battle here when he tried to take a local girl for his wife.

South-east, in County Down near the borders with the Republic, are the lovely Mourne Mountains. Slieve Donard, the highest of the peaks, rises to 2796 feet, and the region has ten other summits over 2000 feet. There is only one road through the mountains, and the area is very popular with walkers. Along the coast, where the mountains run right down to the sea, there are picturesque little fishing harbours, many old castles and ancient and early Christian remains.

County Down is where St Patrick first landed in Ireland. The landscape is characterised by *drumlins,* little hills of boulder clay thrown up by ice sheets as they moved south during the last Ice Age. Strangford Lough, in north-eastern County Down, is a large sea inlet that is rich in all kinds of marine wildlife, including sponges, corals, sharks, whales, seals and a wide range of bird and plant species.

Inland lies Armagh, which Ireland's patron saint, Patrick, is said to have made his base in the 5th century. Armagh is now seat for both the Catholic and Church of Ireland Primates of All-Ireland. At Navan Fort to the west, known as Eamhain Macha in Celtic times, the Celtic kings of Ulster held their court with their Knights of the Red Branch, a kind of Irish equivalent of King Arthur's Knights of the Round Table. Founded by

A young Irish couple relax for a moment during a dog show. Empty Coke cans show the influence of modern consumer society, and yet Irish life remains in many ways extraordinarily traditional. The all-important influence of the Roman Catholic Church has ensured that abortion and divorce have not been legalised, and many Irish women are still very much confined to the home.

Queen Macha, a legendary warrior-queen said to have reigned from 658 to 651 BC, the fort was probably a ritual site, and contains the remains of several ancient tombs.

County Fermanagh is Ireland's lakeland. Lower Loch Erne, dotted with many islands, occupies much of the

northern part of the county. In the graveyard on Boa Island there is a double-faced carved stone figure, with a second figure nearby. Their origin and purpose are not known but they are probably very early Christian. The church on Devenish Island contains a collection of ancient stone heads. Heads were of great symbolic importance to the Celts. They believed them to be the source of the 'life force' and cut off the heads of their enemies in battle. On White Island there are also several early Christian figures in the church. Remote Upper Lough Erne is strewn with uninhabited islands, although ruins of cottages and farms prove that people once lived on these islands. In the past, cattle would have been taken across the lough in flat-bottomed boats with sloping ends, known as 'cots'.

Belfast, the capital city of Ulster, is a strikingly handsome city, occupying a dramatic setting between Belfast Lough and the foothills of the Antrim Mountains. It grew with the Industrial Revolution – linen and shipbuilding were its chief trades – and its character is predominantly Victorian. Rising in the centre is the City Hall, a splendidly ornate affair of Greek and Italian marble. A few blocks to the west is the Opera House, another superb specimen of Victorian architecture – its chief glory being its rococo interior. Queen's University to the south was built in 1849 in the Tudor style, while the Custom House overlooking the

The Irish are keen gamblers. Even with high unemployment and a troubled economy, huge amounts of money regularly change hands at the greyhound tracks of Dublin's Shelbourne Park and Harold's Cross, or at Phoenix Park or Leopardstown horse races. The Irish Derby in June is a big day in the horse-racing calendar – with none of the formality of its English counterpart. It is held at the mecca of Irish racing – the Curragh, west of Dublin.

All the traditional sports are enjoyed in Ireland – tug-of-war, rugby, soccer, even a little cricket in places. But the Irish also have one or two games that are uniquely their own. Gaelic football looks like a strange mix of rugby and soccer – the ball is round as in soccer, but it can be picked up and thrown from player to player as in rugby. Hurling, meanwhile, bears a passing resemblance to hockey – it is played with sticks, or hurleys, but the ball can be caught in the air and carried along the field on the tip of the hurley.

River Lagan was constructed in honey-coloured stone in the Italian style. Belfast's newer buildings include the fine Church of Ireland cathedral, built in a modern Romanesque style.

Belfast's linen trade, once one of the most important in the world, has long since died, but the giant cranes – nicknamed Samson and Goliath – of the Harland and Wolff shipyard that tower opposite the Custom House testify to the survival of shipbuilding. Harland and Wolff (with the ill-fated *Titanic* to their credit) also boasts the world's largest dry dock.

But, of course, there are also constant reminders of the present troubles. It seems hard now to believe that Belfast was once noted for liberal attitudes towards religion. In the late 18th century its Protestants banded together to provide funds to build a church for their Catholic fellows. It was the chief stronghold of Wolfe Tone's United Irishmen, and six Presbyterian ministers were hanged for their part in the 1798 uprising. Decay set in with the city's industrial expansion in the 19th century. This period saw stern fundamentalist preachers such as 'Roaring' Hanna thunder forth damnation against what he termed the idolatrous Catholics, and regular sectarian riots between Protestants and Catholics in the slums of West Belfast.

The result of all that can now be seen in the segregation of West Belfast into the Catholic areas around the Falls Road and the Protestant areas around the Shanklin and Crumlin Roads. And yet, for all the hatred and violence, people on both sides of the religious divide can be extraordinarily friendly and welcoming.

Ulster's troubles have long roots. For centuries it was dominated by the O'Neill family. In the 1590s, Hugh O'Neill, King of Ulster to the Irish and Earl of Tyrone to the English, determined to halt the growth of English power in Ireland and led a rebellion against Elizabeth I. It proved to be a bloody and destructive affair. Promises of Spanish backing failed to materialise, and initial Irish successes turned to defeat at Kinsale in the south. O'Neill's rebellion led in the long run to the very opposite of what he had intended. Elizabeth's successor James I instituted the policy of settling Protestant 'planters' in Ulster, and in the late 17th century the mettle of these planters was tested when another rebellion broke out in Ireland – in support of the Catholic James II, who had been ousted from the British throne in favour of his Protestant daughter Mary and her husband William of Orange. On April 17, 1689, a Jacobite army reached Londonderry. The forces ranged against the city seemed overwhelming. But, in a moment that has passed powerfully into the imagination of the Ulster Protestants, a group of apprentices took action into their own hands and closed the city gates. There followed a gruelling 15-week siege. On the night of July 31/August 1 the Jacobites withdrew (to face final defeat at the Battle of the Boyne in July 1690). Some 7000 of Londonderry's 30,000 inhabitants had died during the siege. In this way were laid and nurtured the seeds of today's problems in the North.

Bricked-in windows in a terrace on the border between Catholic and Protestant areas in Londonderry tell the sad tale of Northern Ireland's sectarian divide. The North's second city – still Derry to the Catholics – acquired the London in its name when much of the land around it was granted to the City of London in the early 17th century. From that day to this, it has seen some of the worst moments in the conflicts between the region's two communities – from the siege of Londonderry in 1689 to the start of the present troubles in the late 1960s.

Norway

The history of Norway has been one of both triumphs and
tribulations. In the early days its Viking warriors sowed terror
across much of western Europe, but from the 14th century
Norway underwent a long period of foreign rule, only re-
emerging as an independent country in this century. Nowadays
Norwegians are among the richest people in Europe. Despite
these ups and downs, there is one thing that has not changed: the
splendour of the Norwegian landscape, whether experienced in
the smile of a fjord or the furious turbulence of an Arctic storm or
the wild and desolate fastnesses of North Cape.

Ålesund, one of Norway's busiest ports, occupies a spectacular setting. The colourful façades of its old merchant homes and warehouses contrast with the blues and greens of the sea and mountains. Everything in Ålesund revolves around the sea and fishing.

Norwegians eat a lot of fish, and the choice is enormous. Displays of fish, fresh, dried and smoked, make a mouth-watering spectacle in the markets of Norwegian towns.

Previous page:
Norway in winter. While the Baltic coastlines of Sweden and Finland are frozen in winter, even in the Arctic Norway's waters remain largely free of ice, thanks to the Gulf Stream.

Fjord Heartland of the Vikings

Few countries have been blessed with a landscape as spectacular as Norway's. The fjords that cleave up to 115 miles inland; the mountains that rise sheer from the northern seas; the remote and magnificent fastnesses around North Cape (Europe's northernmost point), where the sun never sets in summer; the dense green acres of superb forestland: in the light of all these, it is hardly surprising that the modern-day descendants of the Vikings are among the most environmentally conscious people in the world. For they inhabit one of the world's most awe-inspiring landscapes.

Norwegians live in the sixth largest country in Europe – a little larger than Italy – and yet they have a population of only 4.2 million (slightly under half that of London). They are a healthy people, with plenty of unspoiled outdoors to enjoy. But they are resilient too, used to extracting a hard living in a country where less than 5 per cent of the land is cultivable.

And yet today Norway's per capita income is one of the highest in the world. The Norwegian 'economic miracle' was built on the methodical exploitation of the country's physical and cultural resources. These include an ancient seafaring tradition which encouraged the growth of what is still one of the largest merchant fleets in the world; forests which provide the raw material for large paper and furniture industries; offshore seas rich in fish of all kinds; huge tumbling waterfalls for producing hydroelectric power; and, finally, the oil and natural gas resources which fuelled the bonanza of the early 1970s onwards. Through careful planning, the Norwegians have taken a harsh environment and turned it to their advantage. In the process they have built what many would see as a near-model society. Norway is certainly one of the world's most egalitarian societies, with few extremes of wealth or poverty and one of the most efficient social security systems in the world.

As a nation, Norway has experienced periods of both independence and subjugation. The power of the country was at its peak during the first half of the 13th century, when it controlled Greenland, Iceland, Faroe and many of the islands around Britain, but nearly half the population was killed during the Black Death of 1349-50, and in 1397 it began a long era of foreign domination, first under Denmark, and then, from 1814 and on a slightly freer basis, under Sweden. Only in 1905 did Norway once again become an independent sovereign state, although even then it was to suffer five years of Nazi occupation during the Second World War. This chain of events is reflected in the naming of the capital, Oslo. Look for Oslo on a map from around 1920 and you will find no reference to it. Look in a Norwegian newspaper from 1950 and you will find that Oslo was celebrating its 900th anniversary that year. The explanation? Oslo is indeed the city's ancient name, but in 1624 Christian IV of Denmark, proud of having rebuilt his Norwegian province's capital after a fire, decided to rename it Christiania. In 1877 the name was made to look more Norwegian by adjusting its spelling to Kristiania. It was only in 1925, after 300 years, that Oslo reverted to its original name.

The bounty of the seas and forests

Along with shipping and farming, timber and fishing have traditionally been two of Norway's main industries, and are still important elements in the economy. A quarter of the country is covered in woods, although in recent years the forests of the south have come under

In most European countries, shopping baskets on wheels are a practical invention, particularly for older people. In the snows of the Norwegian winter, however, a bag perched on a kind of pushchair on runners makes more sense.

The ptarmigan, or fjellrype, is a member of the grouse family. A thick coat of feathers reaching down to the tips of its claws provides thorough protection against the winter cold of its high mountain habitat. The ptarmigan is a much-prized game bird, its varied diet of berries, seeds, leaves and insects giving its flesh an exceptionally rich flavour.

serious threat from 'acid rain', the result of atmospheric pollution brought in on air currents from industrial Britain and continental Europe. The timber is used to make furniture, in the manufacture of cellulose and paper, and in the chemical industry.

Although it has declined in recent years, the Norwegian fishing industry is still amongst the largest in the world, and since 1945, fish-processing (the freezing and canning of fish products) in particular has become a major export earner. In 1977, the Norwegian Government – ever alert to the importance of environmental issues – established an 'economic zone' stretching up to 200 nautical miles from the country's coastline. The object of this move (which has caused some friction with the fishing communities of Norway's neighbours) was to preserve endangered fish and to maintain seafood stocks.

One of the most colourful events in Norway's fishing calendar (and one that has become something of a tourist attraction) is the annual Lofoten Islands cod harvest. Every year, between January and April, the cod leave the Barents Sea in the north and head for their spawning grounds. These are in Vestfjorden, the stretch of sea between the southern part of the Lofoten archipelago and the mainland. At exactly the same time, some 3000 to 5000 fishermen from Narvik, Trondheim, and even Bergen in the south, converge on the islands to profit from the sea's bounty. The setting could hardly be more spectacular: snow-dusted mountain peaks rise steeply from the sea, leaving small shelves of flat land where the brightly painted wooden buildings of little fishing ports such as Stamsund and Svolvær find a perching place. The decks of the boats are a flurry of activity as some of the fishermen haul in the catch and others sort the fish. Meanwhile, the radar operators pour out an unceasing stream of instructions about the movements of the shoals. In three months of back-breaking work, these men will earn an important part of their yearly income.

The average catch is 50,000 tons. And nothing is wasted. The heads, chopped off there and then on the boats, will later be used in the manufacture of fertilisers. The eggs will serve as bait, or else be smoked. The livers will become cod-liver oil or will be tinned. Not even the tongues go to waste. They are a sought-after delicacy, with a flavour said to resemble that of coquilles St Jacques, and as such fetch good prices.

Norwegians have always gone after rather bigger prey as well. For centuries locals, armed with hand-thrown harpoons, risked life and limb to hunt down whales. More recently, it was the Norwegians who pioneered the harpoon gun and the floating whale factory. Today, however, the whale's survival is under threat and bans on whaling in the North Atlantic and Antarctic have put a temporary halt to the industry.

Norwegian salmon is amongst the best in the world. It is so abundant in the many rushing mountain streams and rivers that it used to be regarded as something of a poor man's food. There was even a time, it is said, when farm labourers specified in their contracts of employment that they should be given salmon to eat no more than three times a week. Nowadays, salmon is valued rather more highly, and aquaculture is an important industry. Salmon has become one of the key features of classic Norwegian cuisine.

Most of Norway's 31 remaining stavkirker *(stave churches) are to be found in the remote valleys of the west and date from the late 13th century, although the earliest go back to the 12th century. Christianity itself reached the country in the late 10th century, during the reign of Olav I. The dragon heads protruding from the churches' gable ends could have come straight from the prows of Viking longboats.*

Dizzy heights and coastal expresses

Sea travel in this country of high mountains and deep fjords remains an essential method of transport. Even if you take a car along the roads that negotiate mountainsides in a series of hair-raising bends, or cross deep mountain torrents over high-slung bridges, you will have to use ferries to cross otherwise impassable fjords and sounds. Local communities are also linked by small, speedy 'fjord buses', and in addition to these, there are the 'coastal expresses' which ply the coast between Bergen in the south and Kirkenes in the far north-east. These expresses call at 35 ports along the way, taking 11 days to do the round trip.

Norwegians, like all Nordics, take great pride in wearing their students' caps. Here, a group of 'academicians', as graduates of the University of Oslo are known, gather for a reunion. Some 10 per cent of college students in Norway continue their studies abroad. The Prime Minister, Gro Harlem Brundtland, for example, went to Harvard, and the late King Olav studied at Oxford.

This pastor is a member of the Evangelical Lutheran Church, the dominant church in Norway. In recent years it has experienced some faction fighting between liberal and more fundamentalist strands. Pentecostalism has also made some impact in Norway.

A nation of seafarers

Norway's seafaring tradition goes back a long way. It begins with the Vikings and their sleek and fearsome *drager* (dragon) ships which ranged across the seas, carrying their families, cattle and all their belongings in the search for farmland away from a Norway that was becoming rather overpopulated. The voyages were marked by extraordinary feats of navigation. Two of the great heroes of Viking exploration were Eirik the Red, who in the late 10th century established the first European settlement on Greenland, and his son, Leiv Eiriksson. According to Icelandic sagas, Leiv Eiriksson led a number of voyages to Newfoundland and to other parts of what is now the Canadian coast, and excavations at L'Ause aux Meadows in northern Newfoundland have unearthed what is now accepted as a Viking or Norse settlement. In the more recent past, this questing spirit has reappeared in figures such as the polar explorer Fridtjof Nansen (1861-1930), Roald Amundsen (1872-1928), the man who beat Britain's Captain Scott to the South Pole, and Thor Heyerdahl (1914-) of Kon Tiki fame.

Today, it is Norway's merchant marine which carries on the old seafaring tradition. Until the early 1970s, Norwegians would point out that the ships of a nation representing 0.2 per cent of the world's population carried up to 10 per cent of its shipping tonnage. Shipping brought in about one-third of Norway's foreign currency earnings and the Norwegian ensign – a blue cross bordered with white against a red background – was a familiar sight in all the world's ports.

As with other European maritime nations, however, high wages and demands for better working conditions for local seamen led to ships being registered under the flags of nations where conditions of employment were less stringent. It was to revitalise Norwegian shipping, therefore, that the Storting (Parliament) passed the Norwegian International Ship Register Act in 1987, and by 1990 Norway's merchant fleet was again the third-

Modern Norwegian fishermen are well protected by powerful cooperatives. The individual skipper-owner is increasingly giving way to larger-scale combines whose trawlers are equipped with the most up-to-date technology for processing and freezing fish while still at sea.

A Norwegian trawler buffets its way through the rough waters of the North Atlantic. The country's fishing industry as a whole has had to fight for survival in recent years as overfishing by the trawlers of many nations has led to a decline in catches of cod and herring. Partly to protect fish stocks, Norway has extended its territorial waters, which now reach out some 200 nautical miles.

'A furore Normanorum libera nos Domine!' ('*Save us, O Lord, from the fury of the Norsemen!*'), prayed the coast-dwellers of Europe when they spotted on the horizon the dreaded drager longboats of the Vikings.

Nowadays, tourists can admire the clean lines of these extraordinary craft, which carried Viking adventurers as far as modern Canada. Examples can be seen at Oslo's Bygdøy museum complex.

largest in the world. Shipbuilding – another important industry – has faced similar difficulties. But Norwegian yards have responded to the industry's worldwide crisis by carving out some special niches for themselves, particularly in the construction of catamarans and oil rigs.

The oil and gas bonanza

It was not without a hint of envy that, in the early 1970s, a number of Swedish and Danish newspapers dubbed their fortunate neighbours: 'Our Norwegian brothers, the blue-eyed sheikhs.' Until then, Norway had long been regarded as something of a poor relation by the other Scandinavian countries. All this changed in 1969 when oil and gas were discovered in Norwegian territorial waters in sufficient quantities to be commercially exploitable. In addition to that, Norway is one of the world's largest producers of hydroelectricity – a key source of energy for its metallurgical industries.

The price of success

Despite these developments, the people of Norway are not universally contented. 'We may be the sheikhs of the North, but we still don't like to write out cheques at petrol stations', complains one travelling salesman. 'We

Weighing the catch. Norway exports fish to the four corners of the world, even to countries with their own fishing industries. These cod, for example, may end up dried and salted on a Portuguese table as bacalhau, a great favourite with Portugal's own fishermen, who specialise more in octopus, squid and sardines.

Scandinavian children have long been accustomed to spending part of their school holidays working. Here, in the Lofoten islands, children regularly help in the processing of cods' tongues, considered a great delicacy by many.

pay more for our fuel than the Germans do for theirs. For a country which produces ten times what it consumes, that's scandalous!' The cost of living is notoriously high, although patriotic Norwegians, sensitive to their reputation for inflated prices, will point out that for the visitor, at least, expenses need not be too high: visiting a museum, for example, is sometimes free, and will never cost you more than between £1 and £3. Norwegians benefit from one of the most sophisticated and generous welfare systems in the world, but at a price, for they also pay some of the highest taxes in the world.

To the outsider, the level of state intervention in everyday life can be bewildering, with its concern – albeit benevolent – to protect citizens not only from each other but also from themselves. Take the state monopoly on the sale of alcohol, for example. Not content with selling it at prices that in other countries would be regarded as exorbitant, the state also regulates the way in which it is sold. Spirits and wine are available only at outlets belonging to the State Liquor Monopoly (Vinmonopolet), which sells nothing else. Beer is available in grocers and supermarkets. Even stranger, to the majority of foreigners, is the law in Norway which prevents parents from smacking their children on the pain of prosecution.

Battles of right and left

'Be like Gro. Choose a man of the right.' These are the words of the Conservative slogan daubed in black letters on the walls of Oslo University during the general election campaign of October 1981. It is a good example of the type of consensus politics that have dominated Norwegian government. For Gro, the diminutive and dynamic leader of the centre-left Labour Party, is also Mrs Harlem Brundtland. And the man of the right is her husband Arne, who until recently was a member of the opposition Conservative Party.

It is Gro's party, which now promotes a moderate form of socialism, that has dominated the Norwegian Government since the war and which can be said to represent the Establishment. Gro has been its leader since February 1981, when she took over from the previous Labour premier, to become the first woman to hold such high office in Norway. Her husband Arne, however, does not pull his punches. During the 1981 campaign, he was in the habit of declaring: 'Bah! If a Labour government bites the dust, that isn't in itself a great catastrophe.'

In October 1981 Gro and her party did indeed bite the dust, losing power to a centre-right coalition headed by the Conservatives. Despite this setback, Gro has remained the towering figure of Norwegian politics during the 1980s and '90s. She was back in power from 1986 to 1989 and then again in November 1990. She is, in many ways, a highly representative Norwegian figure, with a concern for typically Norwegian issues. In her second administration she hit the world's headlines by choosing its first 'sexually balanced' government: nearly half its members were women, a standard followed by later cabinets. She has also made her mark internationally for her interest in environmental issues. From 1984 she headed the United Nations' Brundtland Commission on the environment and development.

Despite its strongly left-wing tradition, Norway is devoted to its monarchy. A recent poll found support running at well over 90 per cent. Norwegians seem to

A family group watches a small trawler set off for the hunt. The paint may be peeling from the wood-built houses lining the quay, but inside they have every modern comfort, including, of course, freezers to store the owners' share of the catch.

adore their royal family, and even the tiny republican minority have a hard time finding anything critical to say about them. From the very start, members of the present royal family have been models of democratic constitutionalism. There have been only three monarchs since Norway won its independence in 1905, when the first king, Haakon VII, a Danish prince by birth and son-in-law of Britain's Edward VII, was elected to the throne in a popular referendum. This was held at his own insistence, otherwise he would not have accepted the offer of the crown. He watched over his country's fortunes for 52 years – a reign which encompassed the bitter years of German occupation in the Second World War, when from exile in England he did much to keep alive the spirit of Norwegian resistance. His son, the bluff Olav V, was like a much-loved father to the nation at large. The present king, Harald V, who came to the throne in 1991, was educated at local state schools like any other Norwegian and has the distinction of being the first Norwegian king to be born in his country since the Middle Ages.

On the beautiful island of Senja, north of the Lofotens, jagged, snow-patched mountains rise from the sea, leaving a narrow, green strip at their feet. Norway's coastline boasts some 50,000 islands, of which Senja is one of the largest.

Norwegian spoken ... and Norwegian

Norway's history of foreign domination explains one of its linguistic quirks: two versions of the same language have equal status as the country's official tongue. During the centuries of rule from Copenhagen, Danish, rather than any local form of speech, was the language of commerce, the church and administration.

Then, in the 19th century, at a time of renewed interest in national and regional traditions throughout Europe, the self-taught scholar Ivar Aasen (1813-96), a herbalist by training, undertook the task of studying the Norwegian language and its development. He visited the remote valleys of western and central Norway, listened to the peasants and collected specimens of their language, including words, inflections and sound patterns. Then, using the information he had gathered, he set about reconstituting a national language, codifying its grammar and compiling a dictionary. Although Sweden ruled Norway at that time, it allowed the country a large measure of internal self rule, and in 1885 the Norwegian Storting decided that the Norwegian language *landsmaal* should have equal status with Dano-Norwegian. In the 1920s, Aasen's language was renamed *nynorsk* (modern Norwegian), in order to distinguish it from Dano-Norwegian, now called *bokmål* (the language of books).

In everyday life, being bilingual can, to some extent, complicate matters. It means, for example, that the country has two names: *Norge* in *bokmål* and *Noreg* in *nynorsk*. Most schools teach in *bokmål*, but a sizeable minority use *nynorsk*. In the eastern, more heavily populated part of the country (which includes Oslo), *bokmål* is used most frequently, whereas *nynorsk* is strongest in the rural western parts. In practice, however, the two languages create few real problems. Given the fact that Danes, Swedes and Norwegians are able to communicate with one another, each in their own language, there are unlikely to be difficulties between speakers of *bokmål* and *nynorsk*.

The stabbur *is the outside larder where Norwegian families traditionally stored their provisions for the winter. It stands near the house and is built on pilings in order to protect its contents from rodents and damp. In many cases, grass grows on the thatched roof, providing an extra layer of protection.*

A neatly painted farmhouse presents a surprisingly domestic scene at the foot of a rugged precipice rising above Hardangerfjord, east of Bergen. About a third of all Norway's farms are, like this one, dairy farms. Cattle are reared in all parts of the country, even the far north.

Fine old merchant houses line the quay of Bergen's inner harbour, testifying to the port's centuries-old prosperity and its former links with the Hanseatic League. The only drawback to Norway's second city and fishing capital is its climate: the average annual rainfall is nearly 80 inches.
An apocryphal story is told of a Bergen skipper who, returning to his home port on a sunny day, thought he had made a mistake and ordered his ship to turn back.

Oslo – the rural capital

The Norwegian capital has never claimed to be an architectural showpiece, having been for so long little more than another provincial city. It is without doubt, however, a pleasantly relaxed and spacious place to live in and to visit. The official boundaries of Oslo extend far beyond the city itself. Thus, over and above its 460,000 human inhabitants, the capital can boast a large population of livestock, not to mention elks and deer.

Arriving in Oslo by train, rather than by road, may result in some initial disappointment. As you emerge from Sentralbanestasjonen (the central station), you will be facing Karl Johans Gate, named after the Napoleonic Marshal Bernadotte, who, as Karl Johan XIV, became King of Sweden and Norway in 1818.

If you have read in the tourist literature that Karl Johans Gate is to Oslo what the Champs Élysées is to Paris, you are in for something of a shock. At first it appears to be nothing more than a narrow street rising up the side of a hill and lined with nondescript buildings. Climb the hill, however, and the prospect improves. The green expanse of Studenterlunden park opens up to the south, with the National Theatre set back among trees. On one side of the theatre's entrance stands a statue of Norway's most famous dramatist,

Henrik Ibsen (1828-1906), who is generally regarded as the father of modern European and American drama. His square, craggy face, heavily bewhiskered, makes him look rather like one of the trolls of Norwegian folklore who feature in some of his early plays. Opposite stands his contemporary and great rival, Bjørnstjerne Bjørnson (1832-1910), the author of Norway's national anthem, and recipient of the 1903 Nobel prize.

Karl Johans Gate continues straight ahead, with open greenery on either side, as far as the elegantly porticoed front of the Royal Palace. On May 17 every year Constitution Day is celebrated, for it was on this day in 1814 that Norway acquired a constitution of its own. Processions of schoolchildren bearing national flags march past behind bands, while the royal family stand on the balcony above, waving to the crowds. On other days of the year, however, things are generally rather quieter. Visitors stroll past the statue of Karl Johan XIV in front of the palace, and the soldiers of the Royal Guard march up and down in dark blue uniforms.

Traditional 'rose' paintings decorate this interior from Tromsø, northern Norway's most important town. In fact, Norwegian peasants painted stars, horses, roses and all kinds of other flowers to lend their rooms extra freshness and warmth.

Come snow or shine, letters must be delivered – as this postman knows only too well. Though its waters are relatively warm, Norway's interior is snowbound for many months during the winter – making it a winter sportsman's paradise.

Norway's popular arts have traditionally shown an almost oriental love of bright colour and elaborate detail. This sea trunk dates from before the 19th century and contrasts with modern designs, which tend to be simpler and more restrained.

Turn left by the National Theatre and you will find yourself descending towards the harbour. The twin-towered, red-brick bulk of Rådhuset (the City Hall), which was completed in 1950, looms in front. Nearby, on the harbourside, is Aker Brygge (Dockland), an area of gleaming modern buildings and strange monolithic fountains. In the evenings the cafés and restaurants here are a favourite haunt of the young and fashionable. Across the harbour from Aker Brygge rise the turrets of one of Oslo's oldest buildings, Akershus Fortress, which was built in the 14th century, although it has been rebuilt several times since. During the war it was one of the headquarters of the Nazis, who ruled the country with the help of their puppet minister-president, the infamous Vidkun Quisling.

The cycle of life

Another place to head for is Vigeland Sculpture Park in Oslo's north-western suburbs. The sculptor Adolf Gustav Vigeland (1869-1943) spent 40 years here, constructing, at the city's expense, this astonishing, and to many eyes, bizarre, glorification of 'the cycle of life'. The centrepiece, which rises from the crest of a small hill, is a huge, heavily carved 60-foot monolith, hewn out of a single piece of stone and weighing 200 tons. Scattered around the rest of the 100 acres of parkland are a multitude of sculptural groups, containing 650 statues in all. They depict the ages of man from birth, through youth, maturity and old age, to death. They have a distinctive, primitive quality; indeed, and perhaps a little unkindly, Adolf Vigeland has been called the Neanderthal Rodin. Babies who look like huge barrels, women with thighs the size of horses', men who wear their virility like a decoration – nothing is missing, except perhaps some fig leaves.

A visit to the Edvard Munch Museum on the other

The sleek lines of this boat are reminiscent of those of the old Viking drager ships. The rocks in the background are typical of the debris left by glaciers in the Hardanger region of Norway and often stretch for miles on end. Not far from here are the 600-foot Vøringfoss falls, among the most famous of Norway's many spectacular waterfalls.

A family of cross-country skiers make their way across the snowy heights. Even their baby joins the expedition, his carriage towed by two dogs. Morgedal, in the Telemark region south-west of Oslo, claims to be the birthplace of the modern sport of skiing, and a statue there commemorates the sport's 19th-century pioneer, Sondre Nordheim.

side of Oslo brings things down to a more melancholy level. Munch (1863-1944), father of the Expressionist movement, was one of the most important of modern artists, but he could hardly be accused of celebrating the joy of living. 'The black angels of sickness and madness,' he wrote, 'stood guard near my cradle.' The very titles of his paintings reveal his state of mind: *Anxiety, The Sick Child, The Scream* and so on.

A short ferry ride from the quay in front of City Hall takes you to the complex of museums at Bygdøy. Here you can visit Fram, the ship used by Nansen for his polar explorations, and examine the craft on which Thor Heyerdahl made two of his astonishing oceanic voyages: the balsa raft *Kon Tiki*, aboard which he and five companions made their way in 1947 from Callao in Peru to the Tuamotu Islands; and the papyrus boat,

Ra II, on which he sailed from Morocco to Barbados in 1970. Even more impressive, perhaps, are Bygdøy's famous and beautiful Viking *drager* boats – the Gokstad and the Oseberg boats – which date from the 9th century and were found in a surprising state of preservation at the beginning of this century. You do not need much imagination to feel the terror once inspired by these speedy creatures as they appeared over the horizon with their menacing dragon prows and sleek, aquadynamic lines.

Another remarkable relic is the wooden *stavkirke* (stave church) of Gol, with a roof that might almost have come from a Chinese pagoda. The *stavkirker* are striking monuments of medieval religious art, and another particularly fine example is at Heddal in the wild and beautiful Telemark region south-west of Oslo. Sadly, of the original 750 churches many were destroyed by fire or simply left to deteriorate, and of those that survived into the 19th century many were too small and were therefore knocked down and replaced by new churches. Only 31 remain scattered around the country today. From a distance, Gol looks like a huge

In a scene that could have come from the last century, a horse-drawn sleigh buckets down a lane, while in the background people skate on a frozen pond. The snow scooter has, to a certain extent, replaced sleighs – horse-drawn in the south, reindeer-drawn in the north – as a means of getting around in winter, but there are restrictions on its use. The Norwegians' deep concern for the environment means that the older forms of transport are still often used.

scaly monster – the scales being the tooth-like wooden boards covering its surface. Close up, stave churches reveal crude Christian motifs juxtaposed with carvings of dragons whose lineage is unmistakeably Viking, proving that at the time the churches were built, Christianity was still a recent import into Norway.

Where skiing was born

Norway can fairly be called the cradle of skiing. For a long time, skiing has played a major part in the country's way of life, firstly as the most efficient means of getting from place to place during the winter snows, and more recently as a favourite sport. One of Norwegian skiing's most cherished sites is Holmenkollen, lying to the north-west of urban Oslo, where the gigantic Holmenkollen ski jump rises against a backdrop of fjord and mountain. Every year any Norwegians who are not lucky enough to be present at the event stay glued to their television sets for the annual Holmenkollen championships. Competitors hurtle down the jump's long ramp before taking the heart-stopping leap into space. The current record is 364 feet (111 metres), but the ramp has been rebuilt to allow 120-metre jumps. A nearby ski museum houses, among other exhibits, a rock carving, dating from around 2000 BC, which is the world's earliest known representation of someone skiing – a rabbit-like stick figure perched on two huge, curved skis.

Another epic event in the skiing calendar takes place at Lillehammer – the site chosen for the Winter Olympics of 1994 – which lies at the head of Lake Mjøsa north of Oslo. Every year cross-country skiing enthusiasts from all over the world converge on Lillehammer to take part in what is probably the world's most testing ski marathon, the Birkebeiner race.

Around the coasts

There is more, of course, to Norway than Oslo and its surrounding region. North and west of the capital are the mountains, lakes and remote, sparsely populated valleys of Norway's southern bulge. If the landscape in parts of this region looks familiar to those who know Scotland, it is because geologically these mountains are an extension of the Caledonian System of the British Isles. Near the southernmost tip of the bulge is the ancient port of Kristiansand, tightly packed around the mouth of the Otra River. From here it is a short ferry

A Lapp herdsman, wearing brightly coloured traditional costume, lies in his tent on a bed of reindeer skins. Increasingly, however, Lapps are moving to the towns, where they live more or less like any other Norwegian.

A young Lapp girl plays with her dog outside her tent. The growing popularity of reindeer meat has led to better times for those Lapps who continue to lead the semi-nomadic life of their ancestors, following their herds from winter to summer pastures and then back again.

A Lapp girl squints suspiciously into the camera from the door of her tent. Schooling is something of a problem for Lapp children brought up in the traditional way. They are seldom in one place for more than a few months at a time, and there are other difficulties too: the Lapps have their own language, which bears no relation to Norwegian or to any of the Scandinavian tongues apart from Finnish.

Norwegians are intensely proud of their seafaring tradition, and survivors of the days of sail are lovingly cared for and preserved. An affection for sail does not, however, prevent a proliferation of motorised pleasure craft here in the Oslofjord.

ride across Skagerrak to northern Denmark. Follow the coast round to the north-west and you reach the narrow coastal strip of the Jæren plain. This is a pocket of agricultural wealth, thanks to rich soils and the warming effect of the Gulf Stream. It is one of the relatively few places in Norway where farmers can live from farming alone and do not have to turn to forestry, fishing or other industries to supplement their living.

At the northern end of the plain stands the oil-rich port of Stavanger, Norway's most cosmopolitan city, where the old and the new, God and Mammon, sit a little uncomfortably together. God is represented by the city's seemingly countless places of worship. One street in particular – Berglandsgate – presents a near-solid front of mission houses, chapels and churches of every conceivable Christian sect. Mammon, meanwhile, is represented by the gleaming modern buildings from which much of the country's oil industry is run.

Bergen – glories of the past

Norway's second city, Bergen, is north of Stavanger. A century and a half ago it was larger than Oslo and Bergensers still retain a keen sense of their city's importance. They will proudly take you to the central harbour and show you the rows of steeply gabled wooden warehouses dating from the 14th and 15th centuries, when Bergen was a major trading partner of the north German ports of the Hanseatic League. But Bergen's glories are not all in the past. A visit to the city's ancient fish market illustrates the continuing importance of the fishing industry, while the cruise liners and cargo ships tied up in the modern docks show that Bergen is still a functioning port.

Bergen can also claim one of Norway's most famous sons as its own. It was here that Edvard Grieg (1843-1907), composer of the *Peer Gynt* suites and the much-

loved Piano Concerto, grew up and spent many years of his adult life. His father, who was of Scottish extraction, was British consul in Bergen. Every year thousands of Norwegians make the pilgrimage to Grieg's home, Troldhaugen (Mound of Trolls), outside the city.

North of Bergen lies the mouth of Sognefjord and a whole scenery of superlatives. The longest of all the fjords, Sognefjord reaches inland to the base of Norway's two highest peaks, Galdhøpiggen and Glittertind, both of which rise to over 8000 feet. The huge expanse of the country's largest glacier, Jostedalsbreen, cloaks the heights to the west.

Back on the coast and to the north, the town of Ålesund stands near the tip of a narrow spit of land jutting into a complex of fjords, sounds and offshore islands. Despite its baffling geography of land and sea, the region around Ålesund is an important centre for Norway's engineering and furniture-making industries.

Along the coast to the north-east is the island fishing port of Kristiansand, where *klippfisk* – dried and salted fish – is the speciality.

To the north-east, around the open expanses of Trondheimsfjord, the mountains give way to lush rolling pastureland. After the dramatic splendours of the southern fjord country, this is a region of more pastoral beauty, where green meadows are backed by gentle

Traditional costumes have long since disappeared from everyday life in Norway. But, as elsewhere in Europe, many younger people are anxious to rediscover and preserve old ways and customs, and will don Norwegian folk costume for special occasions.

mountains clothed in forests and echoing to the sound of tumbling waterfalls. It is also a region rich in historical associations. At its centre lies Trondheim, whose Gothic Nidaros Cathedral – the largest medieval building in Scandinavia – was built in honour of the saint-king Olav II, Norway's patron saint.

The Arctic north

North of Trondheim, Norway's shape narrows down to a thin ribbon stretched along the coastline, until near Narvik there is no more than four miles between the sea and the Swedish frontier. This is a region of dense forests, few people, poor soils and many short fjords and offshore islands. Although most of the region lies north of the Arctic Circle – Norway as a whole occupies roughly the same latitudes as Alaska – it has a comparatively mild climate. Even in the far north the fjords rarely freeze over, and in the Lofoten Islands, off the coast at Narvik, the mean January temperature is 6°C (43°F). All this is due to the Gulf Stream.

Beyond Narvik, the coast sweeps on up to the more open expanse of the Finnmark region, which is bordered to the south by Finland and to the east by Russia. The fishing port of Tromsø is the most important town in the North, and Hammerfest has the distinction of being the world's northernmost town. Beyond Hammerfest and you are on the top of the world at North Cape (Nordkapp), where the plateau of the island of Magerøy comes to an abrupt end in a 1000-foot cliff. An observatory provides a warm spot from which to view the Arctic wastes stretching ahead or to stare at the midnight sun which, in the summer, hangs like a golden ball just above the horizon.

It is only one final haul from here to Kirkenes, on the Russian frontier. By now, Norway has slewed round so far to the east that Kirkenes is actually on a more easterly line of longitude than Istanbul. Yet even this is not the limit of Norwegian territory: far to the north lies the ice-bound Svalbard archipelago, which includes the island of Spitsbergen. The islands are a wildlife paradise. The coal reserves are no longer highly profitable, but some people live there semi-permanently.

The interior plateau of the Finnmark region is home to the Lapps, or Samer, a semi-nomadic people whose traditional way of life has revolved around the herds of reindeer which they follow from their winter to their summer pastures and back again. Reindeer have always provided their food, their clothing and even their homes, for they make their tents out of reindeer hide. Lappland stretches from Norway, across northern Sweden and Finland, and into Russia. Ethnically, the Lapps have nothing in common with the nations among whom they live, although their language does belong to the Finno-Ugric group of which Finnish is also a member. They are easy to distinguish from the Scandinavian races, for unlike the tall, blond Norwegians and Swedes, they are short and dark. The Lapps can claim to be the region's original inhabitants, having reached there some time around 7000 BC, probably from Central Asia.

Norway's black gold. The discovery of oil and natural gas in Norwegian territorial waters transformed the country's economy. Norway has three main oilfields: the Ekofisk field, connected by pipeline to Teesside in England; the Frigg field, which is shared by Britain and Norway and from where gas is piped to Saint Fergus in Scotland; and the enormous Statfjord field off Bergen, where production started in the 1980s.

Sweden

Sweden could be described as the rooftop of the world –
in terms of its latitude, at least. Visitors from abroad are
astonished by its extremes of climate, by the length of its summer
days and winter nights, and by its vast open spaces which are
among the last true wildernesses in western Europe. The human
geography is no less striking: its social structure is very different
from those in other countries, and its patchwork of pagan
traditions and modernism make it unique. Perhaps these two
aspects of the country are connected, and are responsible for its
endless search for security at any cost.

Gamla Stan (the old city) stands on one of the 700-year-old capital's 14 islands. Stockholm is often described as the 'Venice of the North'.

During the long winters, Stockholmers have to put away the motor boats or sailing dinghies which they use in summer to travel between the 24,000 islands of the archipelago. But there are other pleasures in the new season: pimpla (drilling holes in the ice in order to fish) is a popular pastime.

*Previous page:
The broad smile of this Swede belies the popular misconception that Swedes suffer unduly from melancholy.*

The Land of the Midnight Sun

'Because of its physical characteristics, the Swedish continent is relatively harmonious.' This is how the description of the Swedish Pavilion at the World Exhibition of 1878 began. It may sound a slightly bombastic way for the author, Mrs Sidenbladh of the Swedish Central Bureau of Statistics, to start a presentation of her country. But, in many ways, she was right because the country has developed a homogenous identity, and has produced modern social and democratic systems through a slow process of evolution rather than through upheaval and force.

'How about a trip from Stockholm to Copenhagen?' a Swede might ask. 'Let's go *till kontinenten'* (to the continent), comes the reply – in a turn of phrase reminiscent of the British approach to holidaying in France. Never mind the fact that the Danish capital is, like Sweden, part of continental Europe. The distance that the Swedes place between their country and most of the rest of the world is compounded by the country's latitude – right on top of the globe. Equally revealing of a certain insularity is the question usually asked by Swedish radio of its various correspondents in Rome, Madrid, Bonn or Paris: 'OK, so what's going on *där nere?'* (down there).

Such insularity is justified by some of the facts. For example, in his book *The Scandinavians,* the American author Donald S. Connery states: 'Sweden is almost an island civilisation because the country is surrounded by sea and mountains covered in snow. The lakes give it serenity, the forests which cover more than half the land area give it depth, and the size of the country in relation to its population of around only 8 million inhabitants safeguards it against all indiscretions.'

Sweden is some 1000 miles long, up to 250 miles wide, and has 96,000 lakes and tens of thousands of islands strung out along its 1500 miles of coast. A stranger confronted by such an array of statistics might have some difficulty in knowing where to begin; he would be further bewildered by the fact that neither the seasons, nor the rhythms of night and day, appear to follow any conventional pattern. Most foreign visitors arrive in Sweden by plane at Stockholm. The approach is not particularly dramatic, although you will notice one feature immediately. Stockholm is a city whose boundaries are blurred – where it is hard to tell whether the town has been built in the countryside or whether the outlying province has invaded the fabric of the town. In this respect, the capital is an extraordinary microcosm of Sweden.

Stockholm perches on top of the granite and gneiss rocks of 14 of the 24,000 islands that comprise an archipelago stretching almost as far as Finland. It is

As long ago as the 12th century, Scandinavians used to skate on carved bones and, to this day, skating is enjoyed by Swedes of all ages. The tiniest playground is transformed into an ice rink and at lunch-time workers often find a place to skate right next to their office. Ice hockey is as popular as rugby is in Wales.

surrounded by some of the richest salmon waters in Europe. Since 1973, Strömmen – the waterway which joins Lake Mälaren to the Baltic – has been regularly restocked with salmon, and because fishing is free for all in the Stockholm area, lovers of the sport spend hours in front of the Royal Castle or beside the Parliament trying to catch salmon trout that can reach weights of more than 40 lbs. Naturally, the Swedish genius for organisation is much in evidence. Often, the catch bears a plastic label, which means that it was put there by the Ministry of Fishing. The fishermen then conscientiously return this identity card to the relevant office together with details about the fish's length, weight and the exact spot at which it was caught. There are also great shoals of strömming (Baltic herring) which, in springtime, swim along the coast where the sea and fresh water mingle – in that stretch of water between Waldemarsudde and the Grand Hotel, in the heart of the town.

There are few better places to enjoy Stockholm's supply of fish than the Opera Källaren restaurant, which is partly owned by Werner Vögeli, cook to His Majesty Karl Gustav XVI. A complete fisherman's feast is a bargain at 500 crowns per head. An added attraction of the restaurant is that you can sit right at the front of the restaurant on Strömmen riverside. A superb panorama

In their constant game of cat and mouse with the seasons, the Swedes often take their holidays in the depths of winter, when they leave for the south in search of extra sunshine. The long days and the flexibility of working hours also allow them to benefit from the brief – but brilliant – Swedish summers. Passing the day in a pavement café – as if they were in the Mediterranean – has become very popular with Stockholmers. Here they are, in a café in the old city, with the Church of the Nobility in the background.

over the Foreign Office, the statue of Gustav Adolf II, the Parliament, the old town and the castle are all part of the package. In the earlier years of the restaurant, if you caught a salmon, you could bring it to the restaurant and they would prepare it for you while you waited patiently at the bar.

Stockholm is sometimes known as the 'Venice of the North'. Like many commonplaces, this title contains an element of truth as it is surrounded by water. In other respects, however, Stockholm has very little in common with Venice. The city is no architectural set and there are few art treasures to rival those of Italy. What it does have are some wonderful natural vistas. For example, imagine Fjällgatan – a little thoroughfare on Södermalm, the island which dominates a large part of the capital – at three o'clock in the morning on June 6. The experience will be slightly confusing, because you will not be able to tell whether the sun has just set or

whether it is just about to rise. Before you looms the white silhouette of the three-masted *Af Chapman*, which has been converted into a youth hostel. Djurgården, the Swedish equivalent of Hyde Park, gradually edges into focus, suffused with an enchanting blue glow unmatched anywhere outside Greece.

For a completely different experience, go to Sergels Torg the next day. Sergels Torg is a shopping pedestrian precinct in the middle of the district. Here there is nothing natural to admire, but there is, instead, a style of architecture which defies nature. From 1955 to 1975, this area of Stockholm reverberated to the roar of cranes and bulldozers. All the original houses were demolished and replaced by a concrete jungle, thereby fulfilling plans for a commercial development that had been drawn up in 1952. The pedestrianised streets of Sergels Torg have traditionally been the setting for a whole range of political activities and pressure groups; from

the support committee for Kurdistan or the Swedish-Vietnamese Friendship Movement to anti-apartheid groups and the movement for the liberation of Palestine. In other parts of Stockholm this type of activity has had immediate results. On May 3, 1972, the environmentalists won a resounding victory over advocates of uncontrolled development. Some 15,000 demonstrators assembled at Kungsträdgården to protest against the decision by architects to fell 13 elms in the park.

The old centre of Gamla Stan has escaped the urban revolution. It was once a popular quarter inhabited by artists and drop-outs. It was here, for example, that Swedish men first started to grow their hair long in the 1960s – a fashion which even affected the Royal Guard in the 1980s and produced the improbable sight of unruly locks cascading beneath smart, peaked helmets. Nowadays, the buildings have been restored and houses can fetch extremely high prices. Young people still hang

In summer the streets of Gamla Stan are reminiscent of Barcelona or Naples, although their cleanliness is always a reminder that you are in Stockholm. Before the Second World War, Gamla Stan was a working-class district, but a programme of skilful restoration has transformed it into one of the most fashionable quarters of the Swedish capital and a favourite haunt of antiquarians.

out here during the day although street music is forbidden after 10 pm, and many of the youths move on. Sweden is a country where exuberance is often seen as a sign of drunkenness, and the residents protested against the so-called 'Mediterranean' character which their quarter was developing.

There are several interesting places to visit in the Djurgården woods. The Nordic (Scandinavian) Museum contains furniture and objects dating back to the 16th century. The battleship *Vasa,* also in Djurgården, is a national glory. On August 10, 1628, soon after its launch and after travelling only several hundred yards, the vessel keeled over and sank in full view of the inhabitants of Stockholm. This humiliation was set right three centuries later, thanks to a splendid salvage job that recovered the ship from its watery grave in a remarkable state of preservation.

Stockholm's main attraction – and one of the most interesting tourist sites in the whole of Sweden – is to be

The state in Sweden – a model of social democracy – provides generously for the elderly. Very few old age pensioners live with their children, however; as a result, they may lack in human contact what they gain in material comfort.

found in Skansen Park. No country in the world – and that includes Norway with the folk museum on Bygdøy, near Oslo, and Denmark with Den gamle By (the open-air museum) in Århus – has succeeded in creating such a lively and meticulously researched ethnographical collection. The visitor might get some idea of the general physical characteristics of Sweden from the landscape of the archipelago and from Stockholm itself. But it is the museum which gives the best introduction to the human environment.

In the late 19th century, the founder of the museum, Artur Hazelius, wanted to establish a sort of academy of Swedish life in 7½ acres (ten times that today) of Skansen Park. He was not interested in the rather formal type of presentation then in vogue, but wanted instead to recreate an everyday environment. He successfully managed the daunting task of dismantling, transporting and reconstructing 124 buildings – sometimes as far as 600 miles from their original sites. These include a Lapp cabin from the north, a farm from the south, a

church from Seglora and a manor house from Skogaholm, all of which are furnished authentically. A striking example of this particularly Swedish attention to detail is to be found in the hut of an agricultural day-labourer. Every week, an employee of the museum arrives to fry salted herrings and to hang wet woollen stockings out to dry in order to create the smell of the original house and to prevent the reconstruction from appearing too stiff and sanitised. The museum celebrated its centenary in 1991.

Sweden was, for a long time, a relatively poor country: until the beginning of the 20th century, many of its inhabitants emigrated and, with the exception of

Popular pastimes range from learning chess to pottery. The House of Culture, with its giant chessboard, is just one symbol of a state whose government is concerned with amusing its citizens.

Parents are careful to follow the standards laid down by the state for forging the citizens of tomorrow. The commission for protecting children has formidable powers.

the royal palaces and the big houses of Skåne, Swedish stately homes are not like their counterparts in Europe. They are little more than manor houses (*herrgård*), most of them built during the 17th and 18th centuries in central Sweden, typically by ironmasters, at that time the richest people in the country. The manor house of Skogaholm, which was transported from the province of Närke to Skansen, is a fine example. The building in the middle – the main dwelling – is flanked by two separate wings, and the whole is surrounded by kitchen gardens.

Sweden was not, however, always a poor country. It too, like so many other European countries at different periods over the centuries, has had its moments of military and political glory. In the 17th century, it ruled an empire which included Finland, Estonia and Lithuania as well as parts of modern Russia and Germany. The warrior-king Gustavus II Adolphus, who came to the throne in 1611 aged just 16, led Sweden's armies in a series of brilliant campaigns through Germany as champion of the Protestant cause during the Thirty Years War. By the time he was killed at the battle of Lützen in 1632, his kingdom was the dominant power of northern Europe.

During the minority of his daughter Queen Christina, his policies were continued, though using less warlike means, by the astute Chancellor Axel Oxenstierna. Christina, meanwhile, was to become one of the more romantic figures of Swedish history – played appropriately enough, many centuries later, by her equally intriguing countrywoman Greta Garbo in the film *Queen Christina* (1933). In 1654 she, like Garbo later, found the stresses of her position too much to bear and abdicated to become a Catholic and go to live in Rome, leaving the throne to her cousin Charles X.

Charles X, his son Charles XI and grandson Charles XII continued in the military tradition. Charles XII in particular became one of the most feared generals in Europe, whose campaigns kept him and his armies zigzagging across swathes of the continent, nearly reaching Moscow in 1709 and diving down into Turkey for five years in an attempt to continue his war against Russia from the south. He returned to Sweden in 1715, to be killed in 1718 during an attack on Norway. In fact, his prodigious military feats did more to weaken an overextended Sweden than to strengthen it, and his death marked the end of its 'Age of Greatness'.

A hundred years later, the last king of the house of Vasa, which had ruled since 1523, died and the Swedish Parliament chose the former Napoleonic Marshal Bernadotte as Charles XIV. Despite his French origins, Charles XIV proved a true Swedish monarch; under him and his successors Sweden made steady progress towards democracy, to the point where the present King Karl Gustav XVI can claim to be one of the most constitutional of constitutional monarchs, whose role as figurehead without executive power is enshrined not just in tradition but in Sweden's written constitution.

After half a century of state provision and intervention, many parents accept – and even welcome – the responsibility which the state takes for the child. A network of crèches and infant schools relieves mothers of some of their responsibilities so that they can pursue a career. This may be a mixed blessing for the child – for many local psychologists blame the growth of juvenile delinquency on the break-up of the nuclear family.

The wooden horse from the province of Dalarna and the troll, a forest spirit, may have become tourist souvenirs, but they are still to be found in many Swedish homes. Trolls are said to be fabulously wealthy, and the phrase rik som ett troll ('rich as a troll') is quite common.

The sauna, which originally came from Finland, is called bastu in Sweden. A bath of dry, warm heat, it is considered, quite rightly, to be remarkably relaxing. Despite the Swedish sexual revolution, men and women are still segregated – as this photograph of the women's area of Sturebadet, the oldest sauna in Sweden, shows.

The quiet culinary revolution

On the kitchen sideboard in Skogaholm, a display of casseroles and copper and tin plates introduces the visitor to the history of food in Sweden. It is difficult nowadays, in a country where meals are distinguished by both quantity and quality, to imagine that Swedish food has changed dramatically over the last decades.

An early Swedish cookbook, written in the 18th century, begins with the words *Man tager vad man haver* (we take what we have). At the time, however, Sweden did not have much in the way of foodstuffs to choose from. Stews made from cereals and fish formed the staple diet, with pork making an appearance on special occasions. Fresh produce was scarce, which possibly explains why, even today, when the market stalls are laden with fresh fruit and vegetables from all over the world, the Swedish housewife often prefers deep-frozen food. An Italian diplomat once remarked, rather unkindly, that whereas the Mediterranean housewife slaves away at elaborate dishes in a corner of her house so tiny that it could hardly be called a kitchen, Sweden has the best kitchens in the world, equipped with the latest technology ... for the delicate art of opening cans.

The basic techniques of classic Swedish cuisine consist of seasoning, salting and leaving to hang. The celebrated *surströmming* (fermented Baltic herring) – a speciality of the northern shores of the Gulf of Bothnia – is a good, if foul-smelling, example of this particular predilection. Little fish are put in a tin and left to ferment for up to a year. When the lid begins to rise, they are ready to eat. The tin is then opened and a smell (or *bouquet,* according to aficionados) pervades the room. The silvery fish are then devoured with potatoes. This delicacy assumed its prominent position in Swedish gastronomy during the 19th century, its sudden popularity due as much, perhaps, to the fact that it was possible to make aquavit from it.

The introduction of sugar beet made what had previously been a rare and expensive delicacy readily available, and started a craze which survived the protests of dieticians. Puddings were not sufficient to sate this hunger for sugar, and it was added to mustard, put in bread, in sauces, served with fish and used in countless other strange ways.

By 1950 basic family cooking had still not evolved into anything special; years of affluence had done little more than increase the consumption of meat and milk products. The early 1960s, however, brought a quiet revolution. A growing prosperity and the flair of Scandinavian holiday companies, who were the first to cut prices, encouraged people to travel abroad. Swedes developed a particular taste for Spain, Italy and then Greece, where they discovered new dishes and new products. On their return, they tried to recreate their holidays. Their attempts were encouraged by several factors, including advances in deep-freezing and the speed of transport, which enabled food to be imported from afar, and the activities of a restaurant owner and chef Tore Wretman, who, with the help of the media, embarked on a crusade in the cause of gastronomy. The indifference of many Swedes towards the delights of the table started to disappear, with the result that today you can eat very well in Sweden, even if the prices are generally high.

Church and State

Skansen Park is also a good starting point for understanding the history of the church in Sweden, for the church of Seglora now stands there. Built in 1729 in Västergötland, a south-western province of Sweden, it is representative of rural religious architecture. In the early years of the century, it was abandoned by the villagers of Seglora in favour of a small stone-built place of worship. In 1918, after a dozen years of painstaking

Brightly painted kitchens and dining rooms are a feature of Swedish eating. Despite a clear improvement over the last three decades, particularly in the rising standards of restaurants, deep-frozen food is still for many a staple of family eating.

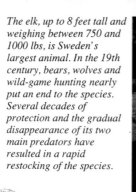

The elk, up to 8 feet tall and weighing between 750 and 1000 lbs, is Sweden's largest animal. In the 19th century, bears, wolves and wild-game hunting nearly put an end to the species. Several decades of protection and the gradual disappearance of its two main predators have resulted in a rapid restocking of the species.

dismantling, the building was brought to Stockholm, where it took on a new lease on life as a rather smart church where some of the most fashionable marriages are held.

Perhaps only in religious matters have the Swedes ceased to conform. No more than a small minority are still active churchgoers, though all Swedes have to pay the tithes asked by the state church as an aid towards maintaining its splendid buildings. Nevertheless, the stern Lutheran ethic is firmly entrenched in the Swedish soul. From it stem the national virtues of discipline and hard work, and the high value that is always placed upon achievement.

Popular Christian belief in Sweden has not, on the whole, been characterised by outbursts of mysticism. Indeed, in his study on Christianity in Sweden, the

On account of its many windmills, the Island of Öland in the Baltic Sea is indeed the Holland of Sweden. Joined to the mainland by the longest bridge in Europe (3.8 miles), Öland is famous throughout the country for a special delicacy – kroppkakor, nourishing little balls of flour and bacon.

A wooden house in Sweden is known as a stuga *and is usually painted brick-red, with white borders around the windows. Stugor range from the most simple of models, which have outside lavatories, to utedass, residences of the greatest style and comfort.*

Swedish ingenuity is often apparent in the smallest acts and artefacts of everyday life. Manufactured brooms may be more effective for cleaning the back yard than the one being made by this woman, but they do not possess the magic of the hand-crafted object. Swedish place-mats are also real works of art.

historian Bernt Gustafsson describes how, in the Middle Ages, Swedes 'trailed behind Europe' and how, in terms of spirituality, 'they are still savages'.

The Reformation of the 16th century was both a triumph and a turning-point for Christianity. On the one hand, the translation of the Scriptures into Swedish by the theologian Olaus Petri, among others, made them immediately accessible. On the other hand, the foundation of a national Lutheran Church was due in many ways by political necessity. When he proclaimed Protestantism as the state religion at the Parliament in Västerås in 1527, King Gustav Wasa was not obeying some sort of spiritual imperative. He needed money to fight the Danish usurper, and the wealth of the clergy (who owned some 21 per cent of Sweden's landed property) gave him the chance to rebuild the finances of the young Swedish state.

In Sweden there is still a group of people whom the cynics call the 'metaphysical militants'. They date back to the 19th century, when many Swedish emigrants left their underdeveloped country to seek a new life in the United States. On arrival, these uprooted Swedish-Americans came into contact with the increasingly popular American Puritan sects. The approach of these cults, with their promises of healing and their visions of a fairly well-defined earthly paradise, seduced the newcomers. On their return to Sweden, these *Svenskamerikanare* found the atmosphere of the national church rather tired and bureaucratic. And so they campaigned for a religious revival, or *väckelse*.

Pentecostalists, Baptists, Seventh Day Adventists and members of the Salvation Army now account for some 4 per cent of the population. They are grouped together under the term *frireligiösa* (free religions – that is free from the state church). The town of Örebro, for example, with 120,000 inhabitants, has nearly 30 different churches, all coexisting peacefully.

Be happy even though you're Swedish

Var glad fast du är svensk! ('Be happy even though you are Swedish!'). This is the slogan you occasionally see emblazoned on the T-shirts of young Swedes, and it is telling because although Sweden may appear relatively relaxed on the surface, society has always been fairly repressed. Relations between authority and the citizen, between men and women, between adults and children were constrained well before the advent of the Industrial Revolution. There is even a Swedish saying which claims that the Swedish family is a place where you live alone in the midst of others.

One of the key characteristics of the Swedish make-up is that – certainly until the 1960s – most Swedes did not care much for the idea of individualism, which they equated with solitude; they were much keener to embrace the idea of the group. It is this preference which explains the success, since the 19th century, first of rural mission-houses catering for believers, and then of the so-called 'houses of the people', which eventually provided a focal point for citizens supporting social democratic ideals. Skansen Park again provides an example of this movement in the Folkets Hus, from Gersheden in Varmland, a province on the Norwegian border. The Folkets Hus is a very simple hut, consisting of two meeting rooms and a little kitchen, where the youth club, the society of 'houses of the people' and the temperance lodge called 'Reform' all held their meetings, conferences, study groups, tea parties and dances. The presence here of an anti-alcohol group should come as no surprise to anyone aware of the problem posed by alcohol in Swedish society.

Take this reader's letter, for example, which was published in a daily newspaper. 'Is it true that

The Skansen open-air museum in Stockholm is a place where people have made intelligent use of traditional homes transported from their original provinces. Visitors can watch embroidery, weaving, sculpture in wood, and all forms of hemslöjd, *the local craft in which Swedes excel. Naturally, the craftsmen and women wear the costumes and headdresses of the different provinces of Sweden.*

Among the dozens of different types of berry in the vast forests of northern Sweden, the hjortron *(Rubus chamaemorus or cloudberry) is the most relished ... and the most difficult to find. If he knew of a secret store of* hjortron *in the marshy undergrowth where it thrives, the Swede would not reveal its location to his best friend, but he would give him a part of the harvest. The berry has a very distinctive flavour and is used in making jams and ice cream. Every now and then, the Swedes complain about the invasion of their* hjortron *lands by Norwegian, Finnish and Polish poachers, who compound their crime by picking the berries before they have ripened properly.*

As the visitor to Skansen and its collection of 19th-century furniture can see, rustic Swedish furniture is quite different from the contemporary style with its clean lines. In general, the traditional Swedish bed is narrow and relatively short. The reason for this is that in the countryside, Swedes used to sleep half sitting up and half lying down.

Bohuslän is a small province situated on the Swedish coast of the North Sea, right next to Norway. It is distinguished by a granite landscape, its scattering of islets, and by a slightly southern feel, which may explain why its inhabitants are considered to be merrier and more extrovert than other Swedes. Fishing – of shrimps and crayfish in particular – is one of the area's main activities.

employees of Systembolaget [the State monopoly for wines, alcohol and strong beer, and the only supplier of spirits in the whole of the kingdom] take the appearance of their customers into account before deciding whether or not to sell them alcohol? On April 17, I went to this shop in my work clothes and ordered seven bottles of *brännvin* [schnapps]. The assistant refused to serve me. The next day I returned in my Sunday best and the same quantity of *brännvin* was sold to me without any questions. Should I conclude from this experience that only "respectable" people are allowed to buy alcohol?'

At the beginning of the 19th century, Sweden was described by one English traveller as 'the world centre of drunkenness'. Alcohol flowed freely and the annual consumption per capita reached 45 litres (as opposed to only 6 litres today). It was then that the various

During the 1950s, the French writer Jean Genet was interviewed by Swedish radio as he passed through Stockholm. His suggestion that the Swedes should stuff their hands in their pockets and whistle gaily in the streets caused a bit of an uproar, because Swedes were not used to behaving in such a way.

The fact that something is not banned does not necessarily mean that it is permitted either. In his memorably titled book *Legislation to the Death*, Bjorn Tarras-Wahlberg, recently Secretary General of the Tax Payers' Association, describes how, over the past ten years, new laws have been introduced in Sweden at the rate of one every eight hours of the day and night – or more than 1000 a year.

A law regulating the consumption of beer and wine at picnics in public parks, a law obliging motorists to drive

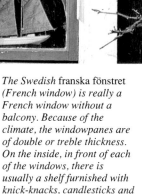

with their sidelights on in full daylight ... and so on. But it is in the field of financial affairs that Sweden really breaks all the records. Mushrooms and berries abound in the woods of Sweden, and the Swedes make a little pocket money by picking and selling them. The authorities, however, decided that too many people were avoiding tax on these earnings and passed a law in 1979 stipulating that any berries picked for sale with a value of over 3000 crowns were taxable, and that the buyer should note the name and address of the seller and pass them on to the revenue officers. The result of this curious piece of legislation was that in 1979 and 1980, local jam manufacturers had to import whortleberries and bilberries while tons of berries withered unpicked in the country's woods.

The Swedish franska fönstret *(French window) is really a French window without a balcony. Because of the climate, the windowpanes are of double or treble thickness. On the inside, in front of each of the windows, there is usually a shelf furnished with knick-knacks, candlesticks and house plants.*

A weekly Swedish ritual – the dusting down of the carpets – takes place in Skellefteå, a port situated in the north of the Gulf of Bothnia. Many buildings in the country have their own space reserved for this purpose. The carpets here are trasmattor – *carpets with tassels made from small pieces of different-coloured material.*

temperance movements were founded. Their initiatives were, in turn, supported by the state, which gradually began to introduce restrictions. In 1922, a referendum was held on total prohibition, 49 per cent voting in favour of the ban and 51 per cent against. Despite the result, the authorities decided to deny the wishes of the people and to do what was good for them instead. The ration card, or *motbok*, was introduced. This allowed each adult a monthly amount of spirits, which ranged from 1 to 3 litres according to age, sex and income; the sale of wine was not subjected to any restrictions, since it was so unpopular. When the *motbok* was abolished in 1955, there was no noticeable growth in alcohol consumption. This should not be ascribed exclusively to the Swedes' sense of good citizenship, however, since deliberately high prices continued to exert an equally restraining influence.

Why the Swedish model?

During the 1960s, Sweden's social system was the envy of the world. Now deep into its second century without war, with a living standard higher than that of the United States, and with one of the most extensive social welfare programmes in the world, Sweden is still in many respects the envy of Europe.

Sweden has had its fair share of luck since 1930. In particular, the country benefited from its wartime neutrality. During the war, Sweden traded with Germany. Then, afterwards, its industry took advantage of the fact that other European countries were having to rebuild their industries. This allowed Sweden to embark on some expensive social innovations. But earthly paradises do not come cheaply, and the Swedes carry the world's heaviest tax burden of up to 50 per cent, with their welfare services costing some 50 per cent of the national budget. During the 1970s, the country was caught by the recession, and industries suffered because the cost of its exports became uncompetitive. Some people even started to suggest that the level of taxation was not high enough to sustain the standard of state services demanded by its citizens. 'In Sweden, the standards of living are so high that very few people can hope to achieve them,' commented the humorist Red Top.

It is only in comparison with their European neighbours that Swedes notice the deficiencies of their own society. Most Swedes feel that social feather-bedding has led to over-government, and are uneasily aware of a blandness and uniformity in the world about them. But no one could deny that there is a great deal of comfort too.

In medical care, however, a shortage of doctors makes it difficult to pick and choose a general practitioner. Except in the case of emergency, you may have to wait between six months and two years for an appointment with a gastro-enterologist or some other specialist. Yet the Swedes have the most modern hospitals in Europe.

In education, too, there has been some slipping of standards, although the system itself is perfectly in line with the aspirations of its founders. A former deputy Minister for Education, Mr Sven Moberg, has claimed that 'school is not for learning to read and write, nor even for instilling discipline. Its main role lies in teaching equality'. He went on to say that education should 'discourage individualism and foster citizens who are well integrated into society'.

Financial pressures – and a high level of taxation – have created a barter economy. There is even a joke that the doctor treats the carpenter for free, and, in turn, the carpenter makes the doctor's coffin without charging a penny. On January 29, 1976 Ingmar Bergman was in the middle of directing a repeat of Strindberg's *The Dance*

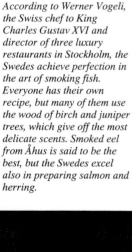

According to Werner Vogeli, the Swiss chef to King Charles Gustav XVI and director of three luxury restaurants in Stockholm, the Swedes achieve perfection in the art of smoking fish. Everyone has their own recipe, but many of them use the wood of birch and juniper trees, which give off the most delicate scents. Smoked eel from Åhus is said to be the best, but the Swedes excel also in preparing salmon and herring.

Gothenburg is the great Swedish port on the North Sea and the country's second city. It was built in the 17th century, in the reign of Gustavus Adolphus II, by Dutch architects, which explains the abundance of canals and brick work. Apart from the shipping companies, Gothenburg is one of the major centres of heavy industry in Sweden: the Volvo car factories and the famous ball-bearing manufacturers SKF are based here. Facing the west, the city has a distinctly cosmopolitan flavour.

The Swedes prepare cod by opening it in two and then hanging it out to dry on racks in the open for two days. No part of the fish is wasted. The heads are processed into manure, the eggs are turned into a cheap kaviar, and the liver is either made into oil or used in the preparation of much-appreciated conserves.

of Death at Stockholm's Theatre Royal, when a policeman and a revenue inspector burst in. Without any explanation they took him straight off to the examining magistrate. Bergman was interrogated for five hours and charged with fraud. His apartment was searched from top to bottom. He was then placed under house arrest and his passport was confiscated. In April, he was allowed to leave Sweden. In an open letter to Olof Palme's government which was published in the newspapers, he wrote: 'In order that the honest taxpayer does not take me for a fraudster, I leave all my money in Sweden. In this business, stupidity and a warped sense of duty have been allowed to run riot. It is a typically Swedish situation.'

In 1977, several months after the election defeat of the Social Democrats, the new government apologised to the great artist and invited him to return to Sweden. For Bergman is as much a symbol of his country as the Volvo factories. Since the 1970s the tennis players Björn Borg and Stefan Edberg, the skier Ingemar Stenmark, the pop group Abba, and the film star Liv Ullman have been among Sweden's most distinguished

The attitude of the Swedes towards matters of the heart has always fascinated foreign observers. Swedes often feel constricted by traditional social structures, and the family does not have quite the same sense of unity that you see in Mediterranean societies. Nowadays more and more young Swedish men and women live together before marriage.

Sweden's network of waterways and lakes has provided an efficient and cheap way of transporting tree trunks. A careful policy of replanting has prevented the depletion of this source of green gold – Sweden has the ninth largest timber industry in the world. Wood is used not only for heating and house-building but also in the paper and match-making industries.

citizens. Nevertheless, Sweden's high level of direct taxation has perpetuated the old problem of how to prevent the sporting stars of the future from following the example of their elders and emigrating.

In fact, the problem of taxation and keeping sporting and pop stars at home is symptomatic of far wider-ranging difficulties facing Sweden. The nation that has for many decades seemed to provide a model of left-wing government at its most constructive has recently been going through something of a crisis. In this, the 1976 defeat of the Social Democrats was a landmark which brought to an end 44 years during which the party had dominated Swedish politics. Admittedly, the centre-right coalition that emerged was bedevilled by instability and went down in its turn in 1982 when Olof Palme and the Social Democrats regained power. But it was a sign of changing times – the consensus that had reigned for so long was beginning to crack.

The next major shock came on February 28, 1986, when Palme was shot dead in the street by a mystery assassin while walking home from the cinema with his wife Lisbet. Palme's commitment to disarmament and peace movements as well as the cause of developing countries had made him a hero of left-wingers and liberals throughout the world. And unlike his peers in most countries he had always refused the attentions of security guards. In view of these factors, his murder seemed all the more shocking, not only to Swedes but internationally as well.

Who was guilty of the deed? The affair remains shrouded in uncertainty and has been a long-standing source of scandal in Swedish politics. In 1988 the Justice Minister, Ms Anna-Greta Leijon, was forced to resign over alleged mishandling of the investigation into the assassination. A year later the trial opened in Stockholm of the 42-year-old drug addict Christer Pettersson who had a record of mental instability. He was duly sentenced to life imprisonment on the evidence of Lisbet Palme who stated that she had seen him at the scene of the assassination, even though no motive was ever found. Pettersson appealed and was acquitted after 10 months in prison. To many his guilt still seemed probable but the evidence against him was insufficient. The inquiry was re-opened.

The 1990s brought evidence of more political shifts in Swedish life. In July 1991 Sweden which for long had kept aloof from the European Community made a formal application to join it. At the same time, the tax burden of the welfare system was proving too much even for the Swedes, while the economic situation was looking ever more severe – government debt was rising, as was unemployment, and industrial output falling. In the election of September 1991 the Social Democrats lost power once again, to a centre-right coalition which had campaigned on a platform demanding cuts in taxes and government spending and a programme of privatisation. More disturbing was the rise of the far-right New Democracy party led by the distinctly eccentric, populist aristocrat Count Ian Wachtmeister, which won 25 seats in the new Parliament. At the other end of the scale the environmentalist Green Party lost all 20 of the seats it had previously held. Clearly, the old liberal certainties of Swedish democracy were being questioned and a new, more erratic era dawning.

Festivals and lights

Traditional festivals are high points of the year in a country where the climate swings between almost total night and endless day, and where the social structure has drawbacks as well as advantages.

On December 13, for example, the feast-day of Saint Lucia, Sweden begins to celebrate Christmas – an event which is celebrated in every Swedish home. The family goes into hibernation from then until January 13, the feast-day of Knut. Imagine you are visiting friends in Sweden. You have gone to bed the night before, entranced by the prospect of tasting a slice of Scandinavian life. You are woken at six o'clock by a chorus of solemn voices on the radio and, rather apprehensive, you open your eyes gingerly to catch a surprise glimpse of the daughter of the house. Her silhouette is blurred by a white and spectral gown. On her head, she is wearing a crown of electric candles (wax candles are considered dangerous and feature less and less in Lucia's headgear). The blonde apparition

Tradition demands that the Lucia chosen by every village, business and family to represent St Lucia must be blonde – as is 40 per cent of the Swedish population. For safety reasons, wax candles have generally been replaced by electric ones. When the levande ljus ('live lights') are still used, someone with a wet towel follows hard on the heels of the Lucia.

The past hundred years have witnessed a revival of interest in popular dance in Sweden. The park of Skansen, in Stockholm, is the leading centre for this, and groups – such as this one from the province of Småland – give performances all over the world.

bears a tray of coffee and *lussekatter* (saffron-flavoured buns), for *kaffe på sängen* (breakfast in bed) is a must on the feast of Lucia. The story of the patron saint of Syracuse, who was martyred in 304, arrived in Sweden in the Middle Ages, although carved stones from the Dark Ages prove that December 21 – darkest day in the year – had long been celebrated. St Lucia's Day, therefore, represents the return of hope, when the depths of winter recede and sunny days begin. In less than two weeks light will have conquered darkness.

Now is the time to make *julkorv* (Christmas sausage), *sylta* (a terrine flavoured with marjoram) and, best of all, *julskinka,* ham baked in the oven combining sweet and salty flavours. It is also the moment to prepare *pepparkakor,* biscuits spiced with ginger and cinnamon.

There was a time, however, when December 13 was a day to fear. Crowds of trolls and other tiny malevolent spirits were supposed to emerge, and citizens organised

themselves into masked processions in order to rout this Lilliputian army. It was only in the 18th century that Christian traditions started to overlay these ancient rites; now, instead of vigilante patrols, a slowly paced song to Saint Lucia is sung to ward off evil spirits. On Christmas Eve, horses on some farms are given an extra feed of oats. They are supposed to promise, in return, not to be workshy over the following year. Similarly, a little pile of seed is placed in front of the house for the benefit of the birds. Remembering this generosity later in the year, they will refrain from devouring the crops.

There are rarely any flowers around at Easter. As a substitute, Swedes collect the branches of birch trees and decorate them with feathers of all colours. Winter ends officially on April 30, when giant bonfires are built to celebrate Walpurgis Night, or *Valborgsmässoafton.*

Midsommarnatten (the festival which marks the summer solstice) is at the opposite end of the year to Christmas, and the Swedes celebrate with gusto. In the province of Dalarna, there are almost no moments of total darkness. In public parks, poles are set up and festooned with flowers, and the people embark on an all-night party of eating, drinking and dancing. According to tradition, telluric forces – electric currents which flow beneath the Earth's surface – are strongest at this time of year, which is why dewdrops collected from graveyards at the solstice are said to cure diseases. But there is no remedy for melancholy, a condition deeply embedded in the Swedish soul. And when the party is over, you cannot help thinking that soon the mantle of winter will plunge the country once more into the shadowy world of its pagan gods.

The traditional existence of the Lapp revolves around the raising of reindeer. This animal has for a long time provided the Lapp with a means of transport, with food and with some clothing. Now that reindeer meat has become a fashionable delicacy all over Sweden, the Lapps make considerable sums of money out of it. Those who still make a living out of raising reindeer follow the seasonal migrations of the herds, without bothering much about the national frontiers that separate Finland, Sweden and Norway.

Many Lapps have succumbed to the charms of modern life. They have adapted quickly to the consumer society and now work in factories and forests. The 17,000 or so Lapps who live in the north of Sweden are still proud of their origins, and there are several associations devoted to conserving the Lapp tongue and traditions.

Finland

The most exotic of Europe's industrially advanced nations is a land of paradoxes. It is both part of Scandinavia and apart from it. Of its two official languages, one ties it to the West while the other links it to the East. Right into the 20th century, Finland has suffered wars, repeated invasions, poverty and starvation. But its people's vitality has always enabled the country to overcome its difficulties. For the Finns, the qualities of courage and tenacity cannot be separated, since they are both summed up in a single Finnish word, *sisu*.

Autumn turns to winter. Beneath a tracery of frost, the autumn tints of these birch trees are reflected in the still waters of the lake. A 20-minute drive out of Helsinki will take you into beautiful countryside like this.

At the beginning of the century, the lynx was in danger of extinction in the southern parts of Finland, Sweden and Norway. Now, as a result of a successful campaign to save this 'tiger of the north', it is relatively common. A fully grown lynx measures about the same as a medium-sized dog.

Previous page:
Blue skies, green forests, brilliant blue waters ... any country with more than 50,000 lakes shared by only 5 million people must be a water-sportsman's paradise. The height of pleasure for most Finns is a sauna, then a quick dip in a lake.

The reindeer was first domesticated a thousand years ago or so, until when it had been hunted as game. It then became the point around which the whole semi-nomadic Lapp way of life revolved. The male reindeer has a more impressive set of antlers than the female, but loses them during the winter, whereas the females keep theirs until they have given birth to their young in May.

A Land Unto Itself

If you want to know whether a restaurant bill includes service, *'Sisältääkö lasku tarjoilupalkkion?'* is what you say in Finnish. However good your command of other European languages, including those of Finland's Scandinavian neighbours, you would find it hard to decipher these words if they were encountered out of context. For Finnish is a language to itself, lying outside the Indo-European family of tongues to which most European languages belong. As a result, the language of neighbouring Sweden has more in common with tongues as disparate as English, Italian, Serbo-Croat, Greek, Persian or Hindi than it has with Finnish.

Few countries are more difficult to fit into any kind of pattern than this low-lying land of lake and forest. On the one hand, Finland – *Suomi* to its own people – is generally regarded as part of Scandinavia. It was, after all, ruled by Sweden for five centuries, until 1809, and traces of that union abound, not least in the status of Swedish as one of its two official languages. On the other hand, a number of factors set it clearly apart from the rest of Scandinavia: the different origins of its people, for example, which are reflected in the distinctiveness of their language; and its historical ties with the east. From 1809 to 1917, the Russian Tsars were also Grand Dukes of Finland and, despite a large measure of autonomy, Helsinki came under the authority of St Petersburg, just 300 miles away across the Gulf of Finland. In 1917 the Finns took advantage of the chaos of the Russian Revolution to snatch their freedom, and they have managed to hang on to it ever since.

The complexities of its history mean that Finland can be a difficult country to get to grips with, despite its people's undoubted warmth and generosity. A Scandinavian country, it stands apart from the rest of Scandinavia. A neighbour of Russia, it is distinct from the Slav world of Eastern Europe. In short, Finland remains obstinately Finnish, an unusual mixture of East and West, with a distinctive history and culture.

Language and culture

The origins of the Finnish language are an illustration of just how unusual a race the Finns are. Finnish belongs to the Finno-Ugric group of tongues. It is closely related to the language of Estonia, across the Gulf of Finland to the south, and has distant links with Lapp and Hungarian.

It is not an easy language to learn, although a surface acquaintance might persuade you otherwise, since it ignores articles ('the' or 'a'). Delve more deeply, however, and you will encounter the five different kinds of infinitive ('to be' or 'to do') and the 15 grammatical cases (subject or object, for example). The Finns' insistence on preserving the purity of their language makes life even more difficult, since it means that unlike many other modern languages, there are few easily understood, largely international words derived from Greek. The near-universal word 'telephone', for example, becomes an unrecognisable *puhelin* in Finnish.

The Finns take great pride in their language, which has only comparatively recently become established in its own right. During the centuries of rule from Stockholm, Swedish was the language of government and learning, and Finnish was regarded as no more than a local dialect. Even under the Russian yoke, Swedish remained the dominant language. The 19th century saw a resurgence of interest in local culture and traditions, and the indigenous Finnish language soon found a supreme champion in the doctor-poet Elias Lönnrot.

Lönnrot spent many years tramping forest byways and visiting small communities in the more remote parts of his country, such as the Karelian and Savo regions of

A Lapp herdsman in traditional scarlet-embroidered costume, with his legs encased in reindeer skin to keep them warm, tends a hornless male from his herd. Many reindeer, such as this one, turn white in winter.

the east and north. In this way, he assembled a collection of traditional songs and ballads which he then knitted together to form an epic cycle, the *Kalevala*, published on February 28, 1835: February 28 is still celebrated each year as *Kalevalan päivä* (Kalevala Day). This magnificent work contains several narrative threads, but the most important describes the struggle between two nations, Kalevala – the homeland – and Pohjola (a country of the far north), for possession of the Sampo, a kind of talisman that will bring prosperity to those who own it. The Kalevala proved a rallying point for the revival of a national culture. It lent the Finnish language a new dignity and confidence, and gave an important boost to Finnish nationalism.

Despite centuries of domination from Stockholm, Finland's Swedish-speaking minority – today some 6 per cent of the population – has not suffered an anti-Swedish backlash from the Finnish-speaking majority. From the time of Finland's declaration of independence, its constitution has recognised Swedish as an official tongue. Swedish is taught as the second domestic language in schools for Finnish-speaking children, as Finnish is in schools for Swedish-speakers. In regions with significant Swedish-speaking populations, all signs and forms are bilingual, and civil servants in Helsinki (or Helsingfors, to give it its alternative, Swedish name) must be fluent in Swedish as well as Finnish.

'Our land, our land, our fatherland'

Most countries take some pride in their traditions and achievements, but the Finns seem to take a particular pride in theirs – partly, no doubt, because their existence as an independent nation is still relatively recent, and partly also because they have suffered more than many nations. The singing of the national anthem, for example, seems to be less an act of national self-glorification for them than one of defiance in the face of the wars, famines and other disasters that have so regularly devastated their nation. Johan Ludvig Runeberg, the 19th-century author who wrote the anthem, was a Swedish-speaking Finn – an illustration of how the feeling of belonging to the Finnish nation has always transcended the barriers of language.

One of Finland's major national celebrations is *Vappu*, or May Day. The night before – *Vappunaatto* – is a nationwide festival when people all over the country eat, drink, dance and probably never get to bed. Later in the month there is a more solemn occasion, particularly for schoolchildren who have successfully matriculated after completing their secondary education. In Helsinki, groups of them walk in procession through the streets, wearing for the first time the traditional peaked 'student's cap', which is worn by newly matriculated students throughout Scandinavia as a symbol of their status. The Helsinki processions form at Arkadiaplan, in the centre of the city, at the foot of a statue to Marshal

The copper onion domes of Helsinki's Uspensky Cathedral – the largest Orthodox church outside Russia and Greece – are a reminder of Finland's links with Eastern Europe. By way of contrast, the looming red and white bulk of a car ferry emphasises the country's ties with the West; these ferries ply regularly between Helsinki and Stockholm. A small fishing vessel chugs quietly across the still waters of the capital's South Harbour.

The 'steel forest' is what people sometimes call the abstract monument erected to the memory of Finland's great composer, Jean Sibelius. The 580 steel tubes – reminiscent of organ pipes – are all of different lengths and, on a windy day, produce an eerie music as air passes through them. The monument was the work of the sculptress, Eila Hiltunen.

Mannerheim, the great Finnish Commander in Chief who, during the 'Winter War' of 1939-40, attracted the admiration of the world by galvanising his countrymen into resisting the Soviet invasion. Led by immense Finnish flags – a blue cross on a white background – the processions take the road out to the Hietaniemi cemetery. Here they leave bunches of roses (gifts from their parents and family friends) in front of a huge cross which commemorates the soldiers who fell in Finland's wars with Russia between 1939 and 1944.

In these simple ceremonies, the students recall one of the deep grievances of every patriotic Finn – the loss of a large part of the nation's heartland during the Second World War. Before the war, Finland's south-eastern border with the Soviet Union ran across the Karelian isthmus, just a few miles north of Leningrad (now St Petersburg). In October 1939, however, Stalin was unnerved by the fact that his country's second city lay within easy cannon-shot of an independent state. He suggested a pact of 'military assistance' with Finland that included two proposals: the frontier near Leningrad should be pulled back 15 miles north of the city; and the Soviet Union should be allowed to lease the strategic military base of Hanko, west of Helsinki.

On November 30, without any kind of declaration of

war, Soviet troops, supported by air attacks, invaded Finland. The imbalance between the forces could hardly have been greater: more than a million Soviet troops against less than a third as many Finnish soldiers; more than 1500 Soviet tanks against a few obsolete Finnish ones; more than 3000 planes against fewer than 20 antiquated aircraft. Yet the invasion proved far from being a walkover for the Russians. The 72-year-old Marshal Mannerheim, a former cavalry officer in the pre-Revolutionary Russian Army, managed to extract extraordinary feats of courage, endurance and ingenuity from his men. White-clad ski patrols harassed the invaders at every turn, hurling rag-stoppered bottles filled with petrol, paraffin and tar at their tanks. These 'Molotov cocktails' – used for the first time and named, in irony, after Stalin's Foreign Minister – left the tanks immobilised. Many of the attackers came from the warmer climes of southern Russia and suffered greatly from the rigours of the bitter Finnish winter, as well as from the difficult terrain. Britain and France proposed sending a joint expeditionary force to help the Finns (the Soviet Union had not yet been attacked by Hitler), but this scheme came to nothing when Norway and Sweden refused to allow the Allied troops access through their territories. In the end, the Russians

It is May, the end of the academic year, and a group of newly matriculated high school students make their way down one of Helsinki's streets. They wear white 'student caps' as a sign that they have successfully completed their secondary education, and they carry bunches of roses given by their parents to honour their achievement. They are heading for the Hietaniemi cemetery, where, following long-established custom, they will leave their roses by a memorial cross which commemorates the soldiers who sacrificed their lives for the nation in war.

managed to grind down the Finnish resistance, and in March 1940 the Finns capitulated.

Stalin, who had lost more than 100,000 men, 700 aircraft and 1600 tanks in Finland, made sure that he got his pound of flesh. The defeated nation had to surrender to the Soviet Union 10 per cent of its territory, and to allow the Russians the use not only of Hanko but also of various island bases in the Gulf of Finland. The Finns, however, were determined to fight back. To counterbalance the pressure from Moscow, Helsinki began to make overtures to Berlin, and in June 1941, when Hitler launched his invasion of the Soviet Union, Finland seized the opportunity to join in on the German side.

At first all went well for the Finns. In the space of just three months, they won back the city of Viipuri (now Vyborg) and the other territories snatched from them in 1940. At the same time, however, Finland started to split with Berlin. Finland was interested only in regaining lost territory, not in getting involved in the war as a whole. It refused, for example, to take part in the siege of Leningrad. In June 1944, Russia launched a new attack, but this time it was taking no chances. Soviet forces were now considerably more experienced than they had been in the early stages of the war and, despite brave Finnish resistance (again led by Mannerheim), they managed slowly but surely to bulldoze the Finns into retreat. The Finnish Government, now headed by Mannerheim, saw no alternative to entering into negotiations with Moscow, and on September 19, 1944, an armistice was signed. Finland returned to her 1940 frontiers, but with an additional loss – Petsamo in the far north. On top of that, the Finns had to pay reparations worth 300 million dollars over the course of six years.

Finlandisation

Finland's population in 1944 numbered just 4 million. It had survived the war as a free country and, unlike many of its neighbours south of the Baltic, was to escape the fate of becoming a Soviet satellite. Its freedom had come at a price, however. As well as the territories lost to the Soviet Union, the war had cost the country 87,000 people killed, 51,000 wounded and 100,000 homes destroyed. The government also had to cope with an influx of more than 400,000 refugees from the lost territories. In addition, the 300 million dollars of reparations due to the Soviet Union were payable in kind. Finland had to supply its victor with ships and machinery, including entire paper and plywood-making plants, electric motors, power stations, electricity cables and forestry equipment.

In these circumstances, one thing was clear to the men who ruled Finland. They had to find some way of coexisting peacefully with their superpower neighbour to the east. In 1948, the recently elected Finnish President Paasikivi signed a new 'treaty of friendship, cooperation and mutual assistance' with Moscow. This obliged Finland to resist if an enemy attempted to attack the Soviet Union across Finnish territory. At first, the so-called 'Paasikivi line' was greeted with scepticism

Stalls in the market in Helsinki overflow with fresh local produce: cauliflowers, forest mushrooms and beetroot. Other local delicacies include reindeer, Baltic herring, salmon and eels.

The name on the side of this traditional horse-drawn brewer's dray is one of some renown in the arts world as well as in that of brewing. The industrialist, collector and patron of the arts, Paul Sinebrychoff, assembled the finest private collection of Dutch masters in Northern Europe, including works by Rembrandt, Frans Hals and Van Dyck. He bequeathed the collection to the Finnish state on his death in 1920.

by some local and foreign observers, who saw it as little more than appeasement. One Austrian politician coined the term 'Finlandisation' to describe the process whereby a country abdicated its sovereignty in order to conciliate the Soviet Union. Only later did the wisdom of the policy become apparent, and 'Finlandisation' take on a more positive meaning.

From February 1956 until the end of 1981, Finland's President was Urho Kekkonen, a lawyer and amateur athelete. This former Finnish high-jump champion proved as agile in politics as he had once been on the sports field. Continuing his predecessor's foreign policy, he managed to win the confidence of successive Soviet leaders and at the same time to present himself to his own people as the man who could guarantee their national independence.

One episode typical of Kekkonen's diplomacy took place in 1961, at a time when it seemed from the opinion polls that the President was losing some of his electoral appeal. On October 30 that year, Moscow sent

Helsinki a note informing the Finnish Government that West Germany was preparing some form of aggression against the Soviet Union across Finnish territory. In accordance with the treaty of friendship, the note stated, the two governments must hold talks. In Helsinki, there was panic; meanwhile, on the other side of the world, President Kekkonen was enjoying a holiday in Hawaii. With a minimum of fuss, he made his way home, then set off again to meet the Soviet leader, President Khrushchev, at Novosibirsk, deep in Soviet Central Asia. The meeting was enough to soothe Soviet nerves; the crisis was resolved; and in Finland Kekkonen's reputation as a statesman of almost magical powers was re-established. When the elections came, he was convincingly returned to power. A few cynics wondered if the whole crisis had not been manufactured by the Soviet leadership, anxious to keep in power the man they knew they could do business with.

President Kekkonen would go to extraordinary lengths to avoid any souring of relations with Moscow, although his statements and actions often outraged hardline anti-Communist opinion in the West. On one occasion, for instance, he declared in an interview that 'the Berlin Wall is beneficial to Europe'. On another, he sponsored a law which forbade the export to Russia of certain articles including drugs, arms, pornography ... and the Bible. From then on, Finnish travellers to the Soviet Union would often have their luggage searched for copies of the Bible – by their own customs officials. In 1975, Swedish television broadcast a version of Alexander Solzhenitsyn's *Gulag Archipelago*. A relay station on the Åland islands meant that Swedish-speaking Finns would have been able to watch it, had it not been for the fact that the station was closed down for the duration of the programme. The station was closed again in 1979, for the repeat.

The justification for this policy was its undoubted success. A glance at pre-1989 Poland, Czechoslovakia or Romania was enough to convince any Finn of the value of toeing the Paasikivi-Kekkonen line.

Land of fine design

If traffic jams are a measure of a city's prosperity, Helsinki is a wealthy place. Expensive-looking Swedish, German, French and Japanese cars abound, but there are also signs of a more subtle kind of wealth: one that it is harder to measure by the standards of the consumer society.

Land, sea and forest intermingle in a baffling network of tiny islands off parts of the Finnish coast. The Saaristomeri archipelago off the country's south-western tip includes over 17,000 islands and islets; all of which make for a yachtsman's paradise. Several huge car ferries ply the waters between Finland and Sweden, and offer considerably more luxury than the one-hour flight to Stockholm. For many people, the ferries' restaurants, discos and duty-free shops are an attraction in themselves.

Dairy farming has become an increasingly profitable business, as has the raising of stock for meat. Together these two forms of agriculture are an important element in the economy. In recent years, Finland has also had some success in exporting a number of different Swiss-style cheeses.

The sturdy draught horse is still an occasional sight on the farms of northern Finland. Although most of Finland is low-lying, the north is more mountainous and is covered with extensive peat bogs and swamps, some of which have been drained since the Second World War to create more farming land.

A Finnish housewife prepares a feast. Though generally simple, the local cuisine is varied and imaginative. It is filling too, for there has traditionally been no place for low-calorie diets in this cold climate. Like all Nordics, Finns enjoy all kinds of sausages, pastries and cakes.

It is a wealth that comes from a truly artistic appreciation of life, and it is to be seen, above all, in Finland's world-famous tradition of fine design. A walk through the Kalevankatu district of Helsinki, or through the halls of the great department store, Stockmann's, shows how well deserved that reputation is. On all sides there are enticing arrays of clothes, furniture, glassware, porcelain and ceramics, all created to the highest standards of local craftsmanship, and both beautiful and functional. There is nothing gimmicky about these goods, no slavish following of fashion for fashion's sake. Indeed, products displaying what seems to be a resolutely modern sharpness of line often turn out to have been made using centuries-old techniques.

The multi-coloured *ryijy* rugs are an example. Nowadays, these strangely luminous textiles are sold as mats or wall hangings, but in the past the Finns used them to wrap up against the cold when undertaking journeys by sleigh or boat. Firms such as the clothing and textile manufacturer Marimekko, with more than three decades of international experience behind them, offer further examples of the same approach. Their garments come in a few standard shapes and sizes, but they more than make up for that relative poverty with an extraordinary richness of colour and decoration. The

Finnish design has always been outstanding. This brightly painted traditional dresser – decorated in typical style with flower patterns – would have lent a welcome touch of colour and gaiety to a cold winter kitchen. In more recent decades, the lines favoured by Finnish designers have become simpler with a starker elegance, but the love of colour still survives.

Rice and chopped eggs are wrapped in a rye-flour envelope to make this dish which has, for foreigners, the unpronounceable name of karjalanpiirakka. *Other specialities include the Finnish version of the* smörgåsbord *(known here as* voileipäpöytä)*; a fish dish baked in a rye-flour crust known as* kalakukko; *and reindeer dishes including* poronkieli *(reindeer tongue cooked in a lemon sauce) and* poronkäristys *(reindeer stew). Desserts include tarts filled with wild berries.*

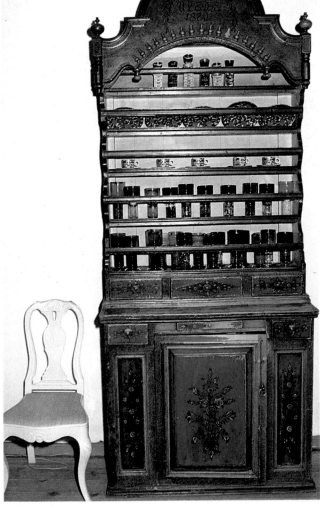

The onion domes of Helsinki's
Cathedral tower above the
North and South Harbours.
It was designed in the
19th century by architect
Ludwig Engel, a master of the
neo-classical style.

clothes are comfortable in a way that shows they have been made to be worn, not just to look good.

The high standards of Finnish design are applied to all areas of manufacturing, from yachts to computer monitors, scissors to armchairs. The industrial group Wärtsilä was a characteristically Finnish enterprise; it built icebreakers on the one hand, but it also owned one of Europe's largest ceramics and porcelain firms, Arabia. Two of Finland's finest artists, Birger Kaipianen and Toini Muona, worked for Arabia. Employees might design tiles in a one-off order for, say, a rich American client, or create a new soup tureen which would be produced and sold in large quantities. No matter what the destination of the product, the standards of design were the same.

The mighty fir

If Finland's postwar prosperity owes much to the high standards of its industrial craftsmanship, another key component in its success has been its forests. Forests cover more than 60 per cent of the land surface of the country, and in these the fir-tree reigns supreme: some 80 per cent of the forests consist of firs (pine and spruce), with birches accounting for another 16 per cent.

The fir has always had an important place in the national life. In the poverty-stricken 19th century, fir-bark was often used in the baking of bread – a custom revived by many Finns during the hard times of the Second World War. Since the war, the fir has been one of the motors of the country's economic miracle. Finland is now the 13th-largest producer of wood in the world. Its complicated system of inland waterways (lakes cover nearly a tenth of Finland) has long provided a cheap and easy way of getting the wood down from remoter areas, although lorries are now the principal means of transport.

Finland takes good care of its forest resources. In recent decades education programmes have resulted in enormously improved yields. However, continuous surveys of forest areas, both by air and by land, have ensured that the timber is not cut down faster than it is replaced. Advances in forestry techniques have been matched by those in the factory. The introduction of new processes and a policy of diversification has led to the production of new types of paper, wallboards, laminates and prefabricated timber components, as well as wood-based chemical products.

Two winter fishing enthusiasts prepare to blow a hole in the ice of Lake Inari, in the far north of Finland close to the Soviet and Norwegian frontiers. The lake, dotted with some 3000 islands and islets, is the third largest in the country. The surrounding region is one of the most remote and sparsely populated parts of Finland, where just 7700 people live in an area covering 6700 square miles.

Culinary abundance

Finnish creative talent is not confined to the production of manufactured goods; it is also apparent in the local cuisine. Make an early morning visit to the Kauppatori market near the port area of Helsinki, and you will be struck by a sense of profusion and abundance more commonly associated with a Mediterranean than with a Baltic setting. Racks of aubergines, tomatoes and exotic tropical fruits lie on heavily laden stalls alongside local delicacies, such as the many kinds of delicious berries

Only the rustle of the pines and the sound of flowing water disturb the peace of the Pallastunturi highlands near Finland's far north-western corner. Once the cold, dark winter months have passed, spring breaks upon the country with astonishing speed. The ice melts, and plants burst into new life. It is in summer that the Finnish landscape presents its truly smiling face.

Cross-country skiers improvise a brew-up in a camp in the far north of Finland, a paradise for enthusiasts of the outdoor life. Cross-country skiers come here from all over Europe to enjoy their favourite sport. Experienced guides lead parties across the snowy heights, teaching them skills as varied as how to wax their skis and the art of camping and surviving in the wild.

Work in Finland's timber industry continues no matter what the season or the weather. Here, a tractor loads cut and trimmed logs in the Vuotso region, an area of forests and marshes in the north-east which is infamous in summer for its huge and vicious mosquitoes. Forest products account for some 40 per cent of Finland's exports. These logs may well be transformed and exported as furniture, plywood or as cellulose pulp for the paper industry.

gathered in the Finnish forests. Meat stalls offer reindeer meat, smoked, salted, dried or fresh. Seafood ranges from the tasty Baltic herring to salmon, from lampreys to eels. Restaurants offer a range of dishes worthy of some heroic feast from the Kalevala: bouillon of salmon, reindeer tongue cooked with forest mushrooms and superb orange-coloured ice cream made from Arctic mulberries. As for drinks: Finns claim that their vodka is incomparably better than the Russian product, and Finnish aquavit is probably the best in Scandinavia.

Helsinki – home of architects

As capitals go, Helsinki is a comparatively young city. It was founded in 1550, but much of the original city was destroyed by fire in 1808. Consequently, it lacks the wealth of buildings and monuments from all ages

Bundles of cut logs float on the surface of Lake Saimaa, not far from the Russian frontier in southern Finland. In a country where 50,000 lakes or more cover nearly a tenth of its surface, floating is an obvious – and cheap – way of getting logs to the timber mills. Saimaa, with an area of 680 square miles,

is three times the size of Lake Geneva and is linked by a series of canals to countless smaller lakes, making it the centre of an enormous water network. Steamers still provide a transport link between lakeside towns such as Lappenranta, Savonlinna and Mikkeli.

Reindeer kick up the snow in a forest clearing while a Lapp herdsman looks on. He is wearing the traditional 'hat of the four winds', so called because of its shape. The reindeer is perfectly adapted to its cold, dry mountain habitat. Its coat is thicker than that of other deer, and its hooves are wider, allowing it to scrape the snowy ground in winter to get at the lichens.

that characterises the older cities of Britain, France and Italy. All the same, this city of famous architects has no shortage of fine architecture.

The oldest parts are built in the neo-classical style, with a characteristically Finnish purity of line that borders at times on downright austerity. The supreme master of this style was, in fact, a German by birth: Carl Ludvig Engel, who worked in the early 19th century. If you stand in the centre of Senaattitori (Senate Square), by the statue of Tsar Alexander II (an enlightened ruler

who did much to improve the status of his Grand Duchy), Engel's astonishing works rise all around you. Particularly magnificent is the domed splendour of the Tuomiokirkko (Lutheran) Cathedral, which soars from the top of a broad sweep of steps.

Following in Engel's footsteps came the great Eliel Saarinen, who worked in the first half of this century and was the first of many Finnish architects to acquire worldwide fame. The most notable of his works in Helsinki is the monumental railway station, built in the

Art Nouveau style between 1906 and 1914. He was followed, in the late 1920s, by a group of architects who developed a uniquely Finnish form of Functionalism, and whose most famous member was Alvar Aalto. This gifted architect created magical effects with the most unpromising of projects, transforming motorways into attractive ribbons traced across green landscapes, or designing tuberculosis sanatoriums as places of leafy beauty. In Helsinki, his most famous work is the huge white Finlandia Hall conference centre, which was opened in 1971 on the shores of Töölönlahti Bay. Another recent addition to Helsinki's architectural heritage, by the brothers Timo and Tuomo Suomalainen, is the Temppeliaukio Church, gouged out of living rock with only its copper dome visible from the outside.

Finnish architects have always been preoccupied with integrating urban architecture as seamlessly as possible into the surrounding countryside. The garden city of Tapiola, which was begun in the early 1950s just 6 miles out of Helsinki, illustrates this principle perfectly. It has become a centre of pilgrimage for architects and urban planners from all over the world, but even for the non-professional it is an ideal place to visit. White towers and ochre-coloured houses rise from the surrounding green. Fountains play soothingly into their basins, and from the terrace of the restaurant in the central block, you can enjoy stunning views of forests of birch and pine, of craggy rocks and, across the brilliant blue of neighbouring lakes, the sea.

The role of women

In 1906, Finland became one of the first countries in the world to give women the right to vote. The following year, Miina Sillanpää became the first woman in the world to take a seat in parliament – in this case, the Chamber of the Russian-ruled Grand Duchy of Finland.

Dried and smoked reindeer meat is a traditional favourite with the Lapps. It is extremely hard, and you need a sharp knife to chip off the flesh. In recent decades, reindeer meat – formerly only enjoyed by the Lapps – has become much more popular in Finland as a whole. As a result, the Lapps tend to sell off the best cuts to the city-dwellers of the south, who eat it roasted or in casseroles, and keep the offal for themselves.

Women have long enjoyed significant rights in Finland. In a sparsely populated country which has suffered more than its fair share of wars and other disasters, it has always been natural for men and women to assume roughly interchangeable roles. During the Second World War, Finnish women even had some experience of military service, rather than only taking on the nursing and back-up roles accorded to women in wartime in most other countries. Nowadays, women are stationmasters, lorry-drivers, engineers, dentists, doctors, even vicars in the Lutheran Church ... Indeed, there are few careers that do not have a healthy percentage of females.

Even in affairs of the heart, Finnish women have an Amazonian reputation for going out and choosing their partners. According to some traditionalists, this has its drawbacks. There does, for example, seem to be a link between the freedom enjoyed by Finnish women and a high level of divorce.

Quiet tenacity

Most languages have expressions that are impossible to translate with any degree of accuracy into another language, usually because they describe a characteristic unique to a particular country. In the case of Finnish, this expression is *sisu*. To have *sisu* is to be spirited, full of initiative and energy, and at the same time to be the kind of person who stays calm in the face of a crisis. It also implies a certain cockiness. In 1939, at the start of the Winter War, some foreigners commented rather tactlessly to a group of Finns on the sheer size of the forces ranged against them. 'Yes!' came the reply. 'How are we going to manage to bury them all?'

These cocksure northerners are attractively impulsive. If a typical Finn meets a stranger in the street, he might well go up to him, offer to buy him a drink, and then spend in one evening what he has earned in a week. On the other hand, it does not follow from this open-handedness that he is a great talker. People tell the story of a Finn who emigrated and then, after many years, came home to visit his native village. A childhood friend invited him for a drink. Together they emptied one bottle, then two. Finally, when they were just about to start the third, the visitor asked a whole series of questions about what had been happening in the village since he had left. Shocked, his host replied: 'Hang on, we're here to drink, not to chat.'

Seen from some perspectives, Helsinki itself can seem like paradise. Technicians posted to the far north of Finland – where the 73 days of non-stop sunshine during summer are balanced by 51 days of uninterrupted night during winter – are paid extra, to compensate for the so-called 'Lapp illness', a kind of nervous depression. People often describe how, during the war, the German High Command was intensely worried by the number of suicides among German troops fighting north of the Arctic Circle in Finland.

Not surprisingly, heavy drinking has been a serious problem in Finland, as for many of its neighbours. It is not that many Finns are alcoholics in the usual sense of the word. The figures speak for themselves: in Finland the annual consumption of alcohol per person is a relatively modest 12.8 pints, whereas France, for example, it is 24.1 pints. Regular drives against alcoholism and a state monopoly on the sale of alcohol have alleviated the problem, however.

The short Finnish dagger, or puukko, *has an ancient lineage which stretches back to the times described in the* Kalevala. *It was a vital piece of equipment, used for cutting up food.*

The bright colours of traditional Lapp costume – above all the ubiquitous scarlet – provide a welcome relief during the long dark months of winter.

Layers of snow provide extra insulation for this Lapp herdsman's hut, while the hole in the roof allows the smoke from the fire inside to escape. The Lapps have learned how to construct their dwellings from the most suitable materials to hand.

The oasis of the sauna

'Holiness is a burning bath', runs a Finnish proverb, playing on the near-reverence that Finns feel towards the most famous of their national institutions, the sauna. In Finland, everyone takes saunas, and there is one sauna for every ten people. A few years ago, the American press made a great play of the fact that after Cabinet meetings, members of the Finnish Government retire to the sauna to receive that almost mystical sustenance from the hot, dry air. The Finnish sauna, rather like Scotch whisky or French cognac, has travelled right across the world. But just as the finest malt whisky is best appreciated when drunk in a certain way, so the true sauna can be appreciated only in authentic conditions and when taken according to well-established rites.

There is nothing sophisticated about a true Finnish sauna. It consists of nothing more than a log cabin on the shores of a lake, and since Finland has more than 50,000 lakes, there is no shortage of suitable sites. Inside, the cabin is heated by a heap of stones kept at baking hot temperatures by a fire of birchwood. Water is thrown on the stones from time to time to maintain the high temperature, though not to create steam, for it is the dryness of the sauna that distinguishes it from a Turkish or Russian-style steam bath.

Finns have different opinions as to how hot the cabin should be – very occasionally temperatures can rise as high as 88°C (190°F). You sit or lie on one of the wooden benches and then settle down to the business of attuning yourself to your body. This is no time for idle chatter – at most, people utter occasional grunts of pleasure and relaxation. Then, when you feel that the time is right, you go outside and, in summer, plunge into the lake, or in winter, when the lake will be frozen over, roll in the snow. Finally, you go into a small room next to the sauna and lie down on a camp bed. Through all of this, you will experience a kind of mental cleansing. Stress falls away, like snow cascading from the branches of a tree, and by the end of your siesta you will emerge into the world a new person, refreshed and full of energy. If you do not, you must be under exceptional strain. As another Finnish proverb puts it: 'Where neither alcohol nor the sauna succeed, there can be little hope left.'

Two Lapp matrons, in full traditional costume, huddle round the central fire of a tent with walls made of reindeer skin. They use the fire for cooking such fare as chunks of smoked reindeer meat wrapped in pancakes. One strange Lapp custom, though now on the wane, is to serve coffee with salt.

A healthy body and mind

The Finns are keen sportsmen and women, and not just of the armchair variety. No fewer than 354 Finnish competitors have won medals at the Olympics over the years – a record which means that this country of 5 million inhabitants ranks eighth in the world for medal-winners. One of the most famous of Finnish sportsmen was the 1920s runner Paavo Nurmi, the 'Flying Finn', with 31 world track records to his name.

Almost everyone in Finland practises at least one kind of sport regularly. During the five long, snowbound months of winter, skiing is the most popular. Skating, too, is enjoyed with any suitable play area skimmed with ice and transformed into a free rink. In summer, Finland's abundant lakes and rivers make swimming the near-universal pastime.

The Finns' sporting prowess should not imply that the people are all brawn and no brain. Far from it. Finns are as proud of their culture and intellectual traditions as they are of any sporting achievements. Most Finns show the same enthusiasm for the theatre or cinema as they do in the sports stadium, and, like the English, they are particularly keen on drama. Helsinki has 12 theatres as well as countless amateur dramatic societies which put on performances of near-professional standards.

They are readers, as well as actors. The Sunday edition of the quality newspaper *Helsingin Sanomat* sells some 400,000 copies every week. Based on the countries' respective populations, an equivalent British newspaper would need to sell over 4.5 million copies to beat that. There is an efficient library system, with both permanent and mobile libraries offering a wide range of reading matter. Books, too, sell well in Finland, despite the fact that they are extremely expensive. For example, the novel *Unknown Soldier* by Väinö Linna, a former engineering worker, was published in 1954 and sold 200,000 copies in its first year – a respectable figure for a serious novel, given the size of the population.

Music also plays an important part in Finnish life. There have been few musicians so widely loved and revered in their own countries as Jean Sibelius, composer of *Finlandia*, was. For a full 30 years before he died in 1957, a large part of Helsinki's annual music festival was devoted to performing Sibelius's works, and the national conservatoire was renamed the Sibelius Academy. Even after his death he was capable of arousing strong emotions, particularly since his music was inspired by a love of nature and the northern landscape. When, in 1967 (the 50th anniversary of Finland's independence and the 10th anniversary of Sibelius's death), a highly abstract memorial to Sibelius was unveiled, many people regarded it as nothing short of blasphemy to the memory of the great man.

Destiny has not always been kind to Finland. Yet, over the last 50 years, it has raised itself from poverty to being one of the world's most advanced nations – judged from the point of view of its economic success, its standard of living, and its creativity and culture. This achievement provides a supreme example of putting into practice that essentially Finnish quality of *sisu*.

Reindeer-drawn sledges are still one of the best ways of getting around in Lapland, though the motorised snow-scooter have been much more popular since the 1960s. The Lapps in Finland have proved much more reluctant than their fellows in Norway and Sweden to abandon traditional patterns of life in favour of the ways of the consumer society.

Denmark

The tales of Hans Christian Andersen, the prince of storytellers,
reflect the spirit of a country where dreamers keep their feet
firmly on the ground. In Denmark the humblest worker is likely to
be a person of learning and refinement, thanks to a system of
education that since the 19th century has been among the very best
in Europe. How to combine social justice with efficiency,
imagination with organisation, beauty with utility ... these are
just a few of the challenges the Danes have taken on and
triumphed over.

*Denmark is a flat country ...
but the greenness of the land,
punctuated by rolling hills
and dotted with cottages and
farms, saves it from monotony.*

*Denmark's farmers tend their
soil with extraordinary care.
Since the 19th century, they
have been among the best-
educated and most forward-
thinking farmers in Europe.*

*Previous page:
This happy young man has
passed the exams that mark
the end of his secondary
education, giving him the
right to wear a special white
cap bordered in red. The
19th-century theologian
Grundtvig founded the 'folk
high school' movement which
opened the doors of
opportunity to Danes of all
classes and backgrounds.*

Land of Poets and Peasant Farmers

'Kong Christian stod ved højen Mast...' 'King Christian stands by the high mast. His arms strike. They pierce the helmet and crush the skull of the Goth.'

These are the words that open the Danish royal anthem. Taken on their own, and out of context, they hark back to the world of the ancient Vikings and give a wholly misleading impression of modern Denmark. For the Danes of today are an astute, mild-mannered, firmly peace-loving people. The country's official anthem (*'Der er et yndigt land'* – 'There is a charming land'), which begins with a pastoral evocation of Denmark's landscape, beech trees, Baltic shores and gently rolling hills, is an altogether more appropriate reflection of the national spirit.

Danes may be peace-loving and pragmatic, but they still have pride in their country. The more pedantic among them will soon point out to the visitor that the Danish royal family, whose present head is Queen Margrethe II, is the most ancient in Europe; that Denmark is the world's largest exporter of pork; and that after the Bible the works of the famous writer of fairy tales, Hans Christian Andersen, are the greatest best sellers in history (a difficult record to prove, in fact, in view of the massive sales of the works of Mao Zedong in China, for example). Danes sometimes even go to the ingenious lengths of claiming the lowest high point of any country in Europe: Denmark's crowning 'peak', Yding Skovhøj, rises to no more than 568 feet above sea level (even the Netherlands has a higher point, at 1053 feet).

In fact, Denmark's strengths are not those of the record breaker. The essential merits of Denmark lie elsewhere. One of the nation's greatest achievements has been to eliminate most of the country's social conflicts and to smooth the rough edges of existence. The Danes have almost succeeded in establishing a society where, in the words of the remarkable 19th-century prophet and social thinker Nikolai Severin Grundtvig, 'few will have too much and still fewer will have too little'. In the process, they have drawn heavily on two virtues practised all too rarely elsewhere: tolerance and the spirit of compromise.

These virtues can be clearly seen in the Danish attitude towards war. In Norway, for example, you can still, with a little imagination, believe yourself to be in the land of the Vikings. In Denmark, however, the fearsome warriors who terrorised much of Europe seem no more than a dim and distant memory. Ask a Dane about his Viking ancestors and his face will break into the characteristic *dansk smil* (Danish grin), which is little more than a gently ironic twitch of the lips. This is because he finds it hard to feel part of his warlike Viking heritage. There is a famous cartoon by Bo Bojesen which illustrates this very neatly: a chubby little man in a panama hat squats on all fours to study his reflection in a pool of water, and to his amazement finds himself looking into the eyes of a fierce Viking warrior, bearded and wearing a horned helmet.

Modern Denmark's pacifism, as well as its habit of self-deprecating irony, is also reflected in the proposal

In Denmark, as in The Netherlands, the bicycle is a near-universal means of transport, a phenomenon encouraged by the small size of the country and its flat terrain (the highest point, Yding Skovhøj, rises to just 568 feet above sea level). Queen Margrethe II herself can sometimes be seen pedalling through the streets of Copenhagen.

Danes sometimes boast, with a wry pride, that their country has more than two pigs for every human inhabitant. They also expound in loving detail on the uniquely long, narrow shape of their sows. Certainly, the quality of Danish bacon is indisputable, the British being among its foremost importers and appreciators.

A red-coated postman makes his way through the cobbled streets of Ribe, a small town in Jutland (Jylland), the mainland part of Denmark. Ribe has preserved its half-timbered houses and original streetlamps. In spring, storks come to nest on its chimneys and rooftops. Wandering through its streets between 10 and 11 o'clock at night and hearing the night watchman call on 'good people to sleep in peace', you might think you had strayed back several centuries.

The island of Bornholm – a rugged place of granite and gneiss – lies apart from the rest of Denmark in the western Baltic. The island's principal town is Rønne, whose inhabitants have traditionally lived by fishing. These lovingly restored old houses are to be found in the St Nikolajkirke (Church of St Nicholas) district of Rønne.

of the idiosyncratic politician Mogens Glistrup. In the early 1970s Glistrup suggested that the country save money by abolishing its army and replacing it with a system of loudspeakers which would broadcast in Russian the words: 'We surrender.'

Denmark has, in fact, been a victim of war. In 1940 Germany launched an attack which caught the Danish Army by surprise. With no natural frontiers to defend, nor any mountains to retreat to, the country was in no position to resist. After 13 Danish lives had been lost, the government surrendered in order to avoid further casualties. It was almost certainly a wise move because it protected the Danish population, including many members of its Jewish community, from the worst excesses of Nazi brutality. As a result, conditions in wartime Denmark were considerably less horrific than those in many other countries in occupied Europe. Unlike Norway, for example, in Denmark a non-Nazi coalition government was allowed, initially at least, to hold power, and King Christian X was permitted to stay with his people. Hitler, who was obsessed with his idea of an Aryan-Nordic Utopia, wanted to extend this arrangement into a complete union of Denmark with the Reich. In a telegram he is supposed to have sent to King Christian on the monarch's birthday, he stated: 'Our two peoples, who are so similar, ought to be led by the same government.' The King sent a poker-faced reply saying that he felt 'too old to reign over so many subjects'.

It was also because of King Christian that Danish Jews were not forced to wear yellow stars – he said that if the Nazis did impose this law on Denmark, he too would wear one every time he appeared in public.

Towards the end of 1942, however, Danish resistance started to foment strikes and acts of sabotage. As a result, the country's privileged status was suppressed and a Nazi *gauleiter* was installed in Copenhagen.

However, for all Denmark's present commitment to peace, its more turbulent past is not forgotten. In 1013, after a series of raids, England submitted to the Danish king Sweyn Forkbeard and the two countries were joined in one kingdom, which lasted intermittently until 1066, when Harald Hardraade's attempt to reconquer England failed. The Danes also settled in Normandy, from where their descendants set sail once again for the British Isles. It is only in comparatively recent times that Denmark shrunk to its present size: Norway was ceded to Sweden in 1814; Schleswig-Holstein was lost to Prussia in 1864 (although Northern Schleswig became Danish again after the First World War); and Iceland became independent as late as 1944. The Faroe Islands and Greenland remain Danish, but are largely self-governing.

Traces of the Danes' links with the Normans of France can still be seen in the appearances of the two peoples, so much so, in fact, that when King Frederik IX, father of the present Queen, paid a state visit to France in the 1950s, the French and Danish newspapers were quick to notice the extraordinary resemblance between the Scandinavian monarch and his host, President René Coty, who was of Norman descent.

Danish design and furniture are known throughout the world, and are the result of a long tradition. Bright colours and cheerful floral designs are hallmarks of Danish style. This is the door to an old house in Rønne, once the home of a prominent local family.

Farmhands and Greek civilisation

Denmark's achievements in the modern world depend to a large extent on its extraordinarily high standards of education. These in turn owe much to the pioneering work of the 19th-century Lutheran bishop, poet and social activist Nikolai Severin Grundtvig, who established a system of 'folk high schools'. These schools have generated such an appetite for learning that in modern Denmark almost everything is taught, from the finer points of economics to the cultivation of tulips or the history of furniture.

Grundtvig founded the first folk high school on November 7, 1844 at Rødding in Jutland. Similar establishments were soon set up in other parts of the country with the result that nowadays all Danes, regardless of age or social class, can attend these schools. No academic qualifications are required, nor are diplomas awarded at the end of the courses. Work is not marked and students are not graded according to their results. They are helped to achieve a higher level of education for its own sake, for practical reasons, or simply for pleasure.

When the folk high schools were first set up, agriculture was the country's chief economic activity and the students mostly came from Denmark's peasant farming communities. In the 19th century, when

peasants in most European countries were illiterate and inevitably limited in their outlook, their Danish counterparts amazed foreign visitors with their standards of education and range of interests. The German educationalist Adalbert Falk has observed more recently: 'An astonishing type of smallholder is formed in the seminars [of the folk high schools]. He sits in his farmhouse, freshly whitewashed each year, his elbows resting on the piano as he talks to you about different kinds of fodder. Then, with a mischievous twinkle in his eye, he watches your surprise as he guides you towards bookshelves where Steinbeck and Maupassant rub shoulders with Thomas Mann.'

Today, farmers represent less than six per cent of the Danish population (as opposed to 39 per cent in 1901). But the 75 folk high schools continue to thrive, retaining their autonomy despite heavy state subsidies. Students can spend between four and six months at these special schools and are given a refresher course at the beginning of term in the subjects they learned at school. They are also taught about the workings of society as a whole, and courses on literature and foreign languages complete the programme. It is a remarkable system where a worker can decide to devote half of his or her time to studying economics, history and literature, while the rest of the time can be spent listening to lectures on Greek civilisation or the social problems of the day. Fees are relatively high, but there is a comprehensive system of grants and scholarships.

The traditional schooling system in Denmark has kept pace with the modern methods developed in other Western countries. Nevertheless, parents are now choosing to send their children to private schools, although even these are 85 per cent subsidised by the state. In this respect Denmark, with its long tradition of social democracy, differs from Sweden, where private schools have been virtually eliminated.

Farmers of the avant garde

Denmark's soil is the country's primary resource. Even though it is of variable quality, and despite the fact that the weather can be very bad at crucial times of the year, the hard Danish soil has contributed to a miracle:

Denmark's fishing industry is still a key part of the economy. Of the revenue derived from the sea, a third comes from the industrial use of fish: in the manufacture of oil, fishmeal and animal-feed.

Most of the boats in the Danish fishing fleet are owned wholly or in part by their skippers, and everyone on board gets a share of the catch.

Danish agriculture produces three times what the country needs and the yield per acre is one of the highest in the world. This success owes much to the flexibility and good sense of Danish farmers in the late 19th century. In the 1880s, when the world cereal market collapsed, the farmers realised the need to organise themselves in cooperatives and also to switch their production from cereals to livestock, and in particular to the raising of pigs. During the 20th century the production and export of Danish pork, beef, dairy products and poultry has gone from strength to strength; indeed, a good 50 per cent of the eggs and bacon eaten for breakfast in British homes comes from Denmark.

In a nation where 65 per cent of farms are smallholdings owned and worked by single families, the cooperative has proved all-important, allowing smallholders to benefit from the advantages of a large enterprise without having to change their way of life.

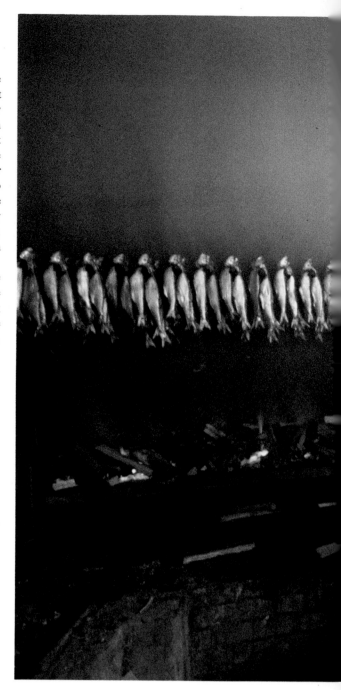

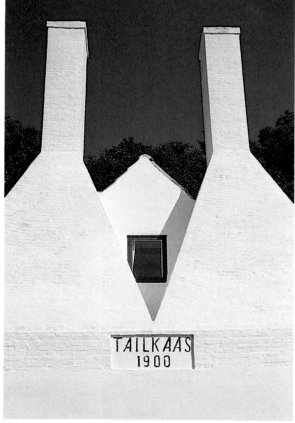

The clean white lines of this fish-smoking plant, dating from 1900, are typical of Danish industrial architecture. Danes are noted gourmets, excelling in the smoking of salmon, eel, herring, sprats and mackerel, which they export all over the world. Denmark also produces lumpfish roe, which is often served as a substitute for caviar.

TAILKAAS
1900

Most smallholders are affiliated to dairy cooperatives, for example. But a typical farmer may be a member of several others as well: say, one for sharing the responsibilities for the purchase of fertilisers and animal feed; one for organising the artificial insemination of his animals; and another for marketing bacon, eggs and livestock.

In Denmark farmland is regarded as an important national asset. All young farmers must study to earn a 'green licence', without which they cannot own farmland. The small farmer is also protected from urban investors: any property of more than 12 acres must be owned by someone whose principal occupation is farming. Even the acquisition of second homes in rural areas is now strictly controlled.

Nowadays, however, all is not well with the state of Danish agriculture. It may be a model of efficiency but, as in other countries, its importance to the national economy has declined. It accounted for three-quarters of Denmark's exports in the 1930s, nearly half in 1959, but today represents just 15 per cent. Indeed, its very efficiency has caused problems in recent times, and the surpluses produced by Danish farmers have contributed to overproduction within the European Community as a whole. Along with other member countries, Denmark has been required to reduce its output of dairy products in particular, and farmers' incomes have fallen accordingly.

Beer professors and Legoland

The Danes have adapted to industrialism in the 20th century with the same pragmatism they showed in dealing with the agricultural crises of the last century. Denmark is all too aware of its small size and lack of mineral resources and has cut its coat according to its

In Denmark, as in many developed countries, people are more and more interested in returning to traditional, small-scale methods of manufacture. This applies equally to fish-smoking, where old-fashioned processes give a more natural product and a better flavour. It is impossible to beat the taste of herrings smoked in this way.

With its many islands and two seas – the Baltic and the North Sea – Denmark would be a bathers' paradise ... were it not for the coldness of its waters. From chalky cliffs to granite crags, from fine sand beaches to green meadows shelving directly into the sea, the country offers every kind of coastland scenery.

cloth. It has focused its expertise and inventiveness on highly specialised areas of industry in order to secure a niche in the world market.

Despite a strong social democratic tradition, the creation of unwieldy nationalised giants has been avoided. In Denmark, all the major industrial companies are in private hands, whilst the state and local authorities run essential public services: the Post Office, public transport, the gas and electricity companies, the ports and so on.

The industrial concern Danfoss provides a good example of the Danes' policy of judicious specialisation. Rather than compete with the Goliaths of European industry, Danfoss specialises in the manufacture of particular parts for refrigerators and central heating systems. It could never have taken on the German giants in the production of entire fridges, but in its own field it turns out a better product for better prices than its competitors. The hi-fi firm Bang and Olufsen and various furniture companies all pursue a similar strategy, producing high quality goods for a clearly defined market. Denmark also has an important

pharmaceutical industry, and is the world's chief exporter of insulin.

Danish construction companies, meanwhile, have done well abroad, building ports in the Arabian Gulf, cement works in Korea and large-scale hotels and hospitals all over the world. Danish architects have been equally successful overseas, most notably Jørn Utzon, who designed the Sydney Opera House in Australia.

In Denmark intellectuals, too, keep their feet firmly on the ground. One of the country's largest companies, the brewers Carlsberg, is ultimately controlled by five academics. The company belongs to the charitable foundation of the same name, and its directors are chosen from the members of the Royal Danish Academy of Science and Letters. Carlsberg is more than just a brewery, however, it plays an important role in the country's scientific and cultural life. Copenhagen's great art gallery, the Glyptotek, which includes, among other things, a particularly fine collection of French Impressionist paintings, was given to the nation by Carlsberg's founder, Carl Jacobsen, and the Carlsberg Foundation also gave Copenhagen its famous Little Mermaid statue.

In this land of children's fairy tales, it is not surprising that toys should have a special place – in particular, the famous toy bricks manufactured by Lego (from the phrase *Leg godt,* 'play well'). A carpenter called Ole Kirk Christiansen started this remarkable business in 1932, in the little town of Billund in the rural heart of Jutland. At first its growth was steady but slow, and after 20 years the company was still relatively small, with just 52 employees. Then one of Ole Christiansen's sons recognised the possibilities offered by plastic, and this transformed the business. It expanded rapidly, so that today it employs over 3500 people and exports its products all over the world, particularly to Germany. Legoland, the amusement park at Billund, is built entirely of Lego bricks. It includes miniature versions of the Amalienborg Palace in Copenhagen, Mount Rushmore and a Wild West saloon, and has become a favourite tourist attraction with adults as well as children.

The tale of the mudguards

The story of the mudguards dates back to 1964, but it could almost have been written by Hans Christian Andersen – except that it involves an all-too-real slice of Danish political life. In the general election of 1964 the Social Democrats had just managed to hang on to power. A number of foreign journalists were in Copenhagen to report on the decline in the left-wing vote, but the Danes had a far more pressing matter on their minds.

It had all started with a decision of the new government to make rear mudguards compulsory on cars. The measure was inspired, as so often in Scandinavia, by the Swedish 'model'. Its object was to increase road safety by preventing stones and mud from being thrown up by a car onto the vehicle behind. Danish motorists tolerated this new legislation at first, albeit reluctantly. But the media and various motoring associations then carried out some tests, which proved overwhelmingly that in rainy weather rear mudguards were themselves a danger and a nuisance, splattering vehicles behind, as well as pedestrians and cyclists, with

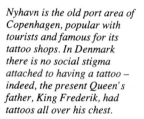

Nyhavn is the old port area of Copenhagen, popular with tourists and famous for its tattoo shops. In Denmark there is no social stigma attached to having a tattoo – indeed, the present Queen's father, King Frederik, had tattoos all over his chest.

Copenhagen's famous Little Mermaid statue has become a symbol for the Danish capital. It illustrates a character from one of Hans Christian Andersen's tales, and was made in bronze by the sculptor Edvard Eriksen. In 1964, the statue was vandalised by some practical jokers who took a metal saw and decapitated the mermaid. Luckily, the sculptor's son had kept the mould in which the original had been cast and the mutilated statue was restored.

In his tall bearskin, this Royal Guardsman might have stepped straight from a tale by Andersen. The uniform of the Royal Guard has changed little since the early 19th century – as befits soldiers in the service of the oldest ruling dynasty in Europe.

mud. Suddenly, the long-suffering motorists lost patience. There was a general outcry which only a ministerial shuffle was able to calm. The author of the measure, Hans Hækkerup, Minister of Justice, was moved to the Ministry of the Interior, and his successor at the Ministry of Justice declared that people could get rid of their mudguards if they so wished.

The story is symbolic, for it shows the extent to which the conflicts of Danish political life affect the surface only. On all important issues, dialogue and consensus remain the rule. Nor is the gap separating right from left in Denmark anything like as noticeable as it is in countries such as Britain or France. Indeed, in 1978, the Social Democrats happily joined one of the parties of the right (confusingly called *Venstre*, that is, 'Left') to form a coalition government.

Feminist paradise

The position of women in Danish society is often regarded with some degree of envy by feminists in other countries. Since 1972, the Danish Ministry of Employment has handed out a leaflet to the numerous immigrants – mostly Turkish, Yugoslav and Italian – who come to seek work in the country. It states: 'Danish law accords equality to men and women. If the man provides the family's income and his wife devotes herself to household tasks and looks after the children, their contributions to the running of the home will be considered as equal.'

Even so, not all Danish women are satisfied. 'As enviable as our lot may seem, inequality between men and women remains a fact of life,' comments a member

of *Danske Kvinders Nationalraad* (National Council of Danish Women). A few years ago buses in Copenhagen carried an advertisement for the daily newspaper *Berlingske Tidende*. In the advertisement, the paper defined its position on the feminist issue: *Pigeløn = ligeløn* ('Women's salaries = equal salaries'). Although these are fine sentiments, the fact is that in Denmark the average salary for a woman is still 15 per cent less than that for a man. Some of the more militant members of the ultra-radical feminist organisation *Rødestrømperne* (Red Stockings) protested against this disparity by boarding buses and refusing to pay more than 85 per cent of the fare.

In the 1970s and '80s *Rødestrømperne* provided the shock troops for the feminist movement in Denmark, and its interests go well beyond demands for equality of pay and opportunity. It played an important part in a wide-ranging debate, the so-called *kønsrolledebat,* which discussed the whole question of the special roles (if any) of the two sexes. *Rødestrømperne* had a reputation for using rather unusual means to make its points. A group once invaded the precincts of a popular Copenhagen café, Hviids Vinstue. Sitting down next to single men enjoying a quiet beer, they started complimenting the dumbfounded clients on their good looks and offering to buy them drinks. The object was to show how unpleasant it is to be accosted in a café by a stranger. The outcome was not altogether successful, however. Much to the women's disappointment, most of the men, after a moment of surprise, accepted the offer: *Ja, tak* ('Yes, thanks').

Rødestrømperne had its own private stronghold on the small island of Femø, which lies in the sound between Zealand (Sjælland, Denmark's principal island, on which Copenhagen is situated) and Lolland to the south. This little enclave received subsidies, as well as the loan of surplus military tents, from the Ministry of Cultural Affairs. Women came here for conferences on various aspects of the feminist cause, and also for an opportunity to relax and enjoy the sun. No males over the age of nine were allowed on the island.

A feel of the 1960s lingers on in Copenhagen, where, in the picturesque setting of a square in the old town, young people strip off their shirts to enjoy the sun.

The Danes are reckoned to be the blondest of all Scandinavians, even though they inhabit the southern-most part of the region. The girls of Copenhagen also have the reputation of being the prettiest of Nordic women.

In 1967 and 1969 Denmark abolished censorship on pornography and for nearly a decade was the foremost exporter of pornography in the world. By the end of the 1970s, however, other countries had caught up, depriving Denmark of its monopoly.

Free love

'No matter how far back you push historical research, you still find the existence of a free attitude towards sexual relations in Denmark,' states Henrik Hoffmeyer, the Danish psychiatrist and lecturer at the University of Copenhagen.

Denmark has played a pioneering – although not always glorious – role in 'sexual liberation'. In an interesting footnote to cinema history, it was a Danish film of 1910 that first showed two people kissing each other on the mouth. In 1976, less than 60 years later, censorship of the printed word was abolished, and in 1969 the Folketing (Parliament), acting on the initiative of Knud Thestrup, the Conservative Minister of Justice, abolished censorship of pictures by a vote of 147 to 25.

Earlier that year, Thestrup, a devout churchgoer, had organised a meeting in Copenhagen's Elias Church, where, in the presence of the church's pastor, he had declared: 'For young people, pornographic images represent no more than the attraction of forbidden fruit. The few people who want to obtain such images should be allowed to do so without the risk of any sanction. I do not believe that the authorities should have it in their power to censor what an adult wants to read or look at.'

The abolition of the censorship laws spawned a new breed of businessman who made colossal fortunes from publishing pornographic material and organising events such as sex fairs. The brothers Peter and Jens Theander in particular profited from Denmark's near-monopoly of 'sexual liberation' with a publishing empire whose flagship magazine, *Color Climax,* regularly sold 11 million copies worldwide. At the same time, the production of 'blue' films thrived, as did live sex shows. Danish tourism did not do too badly, either. Copenhagen's hotels boomed as foreigners poured into the city, often under the pretext of attending unlikely sounding professional conferences.

By the beginning of the 1970s, press officers at the

Copenhagen, the first Scandinavian city to take to open-air cafés, is sometimes known as the Paris of the North. The atmosphere in the Danish capital is certainly more lively and easygoing than in its counterparts in the rest of Scandinavia.

Copenhagen's small boutiques are crammed with knick-knacks of every description and garments of the craziest styles.

Danish Foreign Ministry, embarrassed by their country's reputation, tried to play down the importance of the porn industry, declaring that it was in rapid decline. Although it was claimed that foreigners were the chief consumers of Danish pornography, pornographic material was often as easy to buy in suburbs and remote villages little visited by tourists as in city centres. It was not until the 1980s that the decline really set in, largely because Denmark was no longer the market leader.

The feminist groups played a large part in all this, from the start condemning the exploitation of the female body and, even more importantly, waging war on child pornography, which was finally outlawed in 1980.

Religion in moderation

'In Denmark, to say nothing of the other Lutheran masses, God is irreparably supplanted by what one is supposed to call Science; this Science is no more than an intensive pedagogy, calculated, it seems, to form idiots.' This is how the French writer Léon Bloy (1846-1917) dismissed religion as practised in Denmark. For all that, the Danish Church has produced some remarkably fine and intelligent individuals.

There were early attempts to bring Christianity to Denmark in the 9th century, but these were unsuccessful and it was not until around 965 that Harald I became the first king to be baptised. Six centuries later Denmark, like the rest of Scandinavia, came under the influence of the Reformation, espousing the Lutheran form of Protestantism. In Denmark this was a relatively peaceful transition, with none of the warfare between Catholic and Protestant that wracked so much of the rest of Europe. Nor was there any of the destruction of fine churches and works of art by militant Protestants that was seen in other countries. In the 19th century, the towering figure of the Danish Church – indeed, of the country as a whole – was 'Bishop' Grundtvig. He was a man of great humanity and patriotism whose wide-ranging interests extended well beyond theology and education to Scandinavian mythology.

At the same time, the religious philosopher Søren Kierkegaard's own austere religious thinking led him to attack the established Church of Denmark and its too

If the birch and the pine are most characteristic of Sweden and Norway, the beech serves as an emblem for Denmark. With age, the beech assumes a particularly noble appearance, its massive silhouette topped with a crown of silvery-green.

Fælledparken was once a refuge for down-and-outs but is now a peaceful park where children and young people can play games, enjoy a stroll in the sunshine, or simply have a drink in a café. The tranquillity is broken, however, when the stadium in the park hosts international football matches or large open-air congresses.

comfortable and too secular clergy. In many ways Kierkegaard was a man ahead of his time; his opposition to the idea of absolute truth has led many to regard him as the father of modern Existentialism.

In theory, 95 per cent of Denmark's population belong to the national church, but this high level of membership probably has more to do with tradition than faith, however. Polls show that while only 45 per cent of Danes believe in God, some 85 per cent of children are baptised and some 95 per cent of people have religious funerals. Pastor Kaj Munk summed up the Danes' rather confused attitude towards religion when he wrote of his own parish: 'People here believe in God, not too much and not too little either.'

Pattern of islands

Denmark lays no claims to a wild and spectacular landscape. All the same it is an attractive place, its gently rolling countryside a patchwork of well-tended fields, dotted with handsome stands of beech

'The King's Brew.' This label proudly states that the brewery is a purveyor of beer to the Royal Danish Court. In Denmark beer is regarded in the same way that wine is in France or whisky is in Scotland. It comes in many varieties, from pale to dark, with special brews for Christmas and Easter. The different beers are categorised according to their alcoholic strength; class one comprising weaker beers for everyday drinking, while class three includes the stronger stuff brewed for special occasions.

trees and charming old farmhouses.

This small country – it is only slightly larger than Switzerland – spreads out over the Jutland (Jylland) peninsula and a group of islands at the mouth of the Baltic. In the west, the broad sandy stretches of the Jutland peninsula – the longest beaches in Europe – front the North Sea. Behind a coastal rampart of dunes lie flat, sandy heathlands and peat bogs, many of which have been drained. Plantations and belts of spruce and pine act as windbreaks against the strong westerly winds. The coast here offers so little natural shelter for

ships that artificial harbours, such as those at Hirtsholt in the north and Esbjerg in the south, have been built. The harbour at Esbjerg was begun around 1868, primarily as a gateway for exports to Britain (to which a ferry still operates). Today, it is the world's largest export harbour for butter and bacon, and Denmark's biggest fishing port.

On its eastern side, Jutland offers a landscape of steep, low hills with beech-clad slopes and a coast broken by broad inlets. At the heads of these inlets are small ports and market towns where fine old houses line the sides of gently sloping cobbled streets. Here, too, are the Jutland peninsula's biggest cities, Århus and Ålborg. Århus, once a Viking trading post, is now Denmark's second largest city and port. It has a fine cathedral and houses the country's first modern university, founded in 1928. Visitors can wander through the open-air museum known as Den gamle by

(The Old Town) – a collection of 17th- and 18th-century buildings re-erected in the botanical gardens. North of Århus, Ålborg sits astride the narrows of Limfjorden. It is famous for the production of *akvavit* (Danish schnapps) and boasts Jens Bang's House, one of the finest Renaissance homes in Denmark. At nearby Lindholm Høje there is a Viking burial site which dates from between 650 and 1100.

East of Jutland lies a jigsaw of islands, 406 in all, of which only 89 are populated. The largest island after Zealand is Fyn, which is linked to Jutland by bridges. This is one of the country's most fertile as well as one of its most beautiful regions, with much of the land given over to horticulture. It is often called the 'Garden of Denmark', while its hills, which are less than 430 feet high, are humorously known as the Fünen 'alps'. Most of the towns and villages here date back to the Middle Ages and many have well-preserved half-timbered houses. Some of Denmark's finest old castles and manor houses are found on Fünen, such as the magnificent (and still privately owned) Egeskov Castle. Dating from the 16th century, the castle rises spectacularly from the waters of a small lake in the southern part of the island.

Denmark's third largest city, Odense, is situated in the north of Fünen and is linked to the sea by a five-mile ship canal. It has a museum dedicated to the 20th-century Danish composer Carl Nielsen, one of the pioneers of modern classical music. Odense was also the birthplace of Hans Christian Andersen, and has two museums devoted to the great storyteller.

Andersen's life was itself worthy of one of his own tales. He was born in 1805, the son of a shoemaker. After his father's death, when Andersen was still a child, the boy's mother remarried and then took to drink, dragging her already poor family into ever greater depths of destitution. Despite this unpromising start,

The Carlsberg brewery produces millions of bottles of lager every year, of which a quarter are exported. The Carlsberg Foundation channels profits from the brewery into countless charitable and cultural activities. Copenhagen's finest art gallery, the Glyptotek, was a gift from Carlsberg's founder, Carl Jacobsen, and the capital's best-known landmark, the Little Mermaid statue, was another Carlsberg bequest.

Toddlers clamber over a monumental modern sculpture in the Tivoli Gardens in Copenhagen. The famous amusement park is a paradise for children of all ages – from 8 to 80.

however, a local fortune-teller is said to have predicted that Odense would one day be illuminated in the boy Andersen's honour. And so it proved, although not for a long time.

To begin with, while still a boy, Andersen tried his hand at acting, but with little success. Eventually he was informally adopted by the family of an influential Copenhagen politician, Jonas Collin. With the support of the Collins he received a formal education, after which he began to write plays and poems. He travelled widely in Europe and in the mid-1830s started to publish his fairy tales. Some were stories he had heard

A couple of Danish children enjoy the fun of the fair at Tivoli. The park even has its own brigade of guards, composed of young boys resplendent in scarlet uniforms modelled on those of the Royal Guard. On public holidays, they march round the park preceded by a band, dragging miniature artillery batteries behind them.

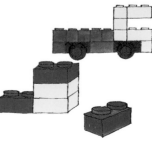

Lego was invented in the small town of Billund in Jutland in 1932. It has become one of the most popular toys ever, and is exported all over the world.

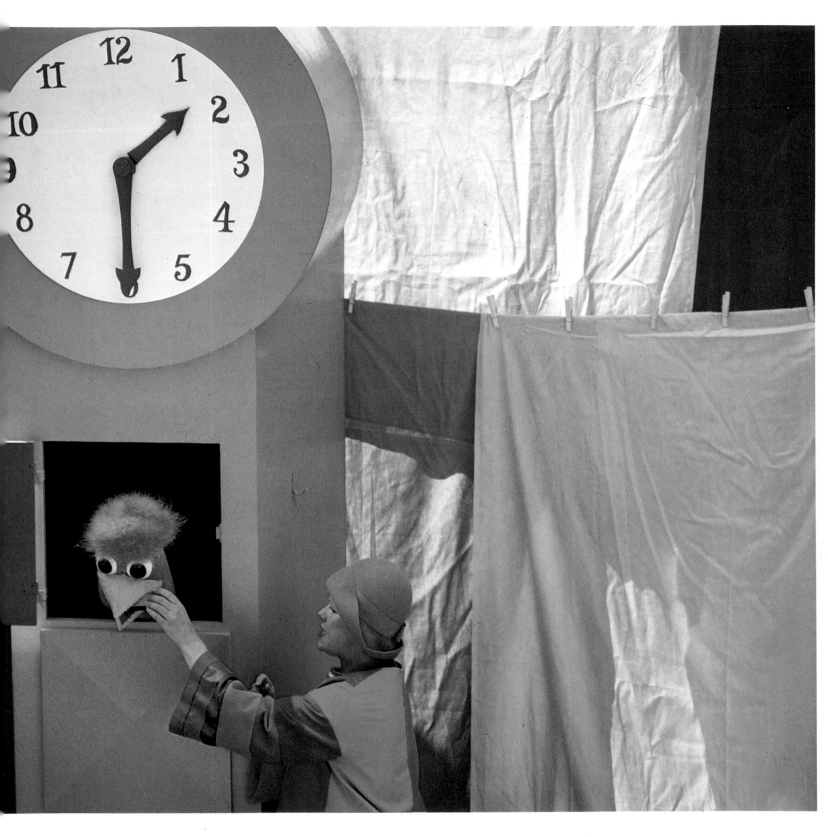

from old women in his Odense childhood; others (such as the famous tale of the 'Emperor's New Clothes') were taken from foreign literature and embellished by him; and a few came straight from his own imagination. But all of them were designed to illustrate important ideas or morals. Although the tales brought him almost immediate international renown, it was not until the 1850s that he received similar acclaim in his own country. By then he was an international celebrity, and by the time of his death in 1875, the fortune-teller's prophecy had at last come true and Andersen had seen his native city illuminated in his honour.

Zealand, the largest of the islands, lies to the east of Fünen. Copenhagen is on the eastern shore of Zealand, far

away from the Jutland mainland, but strategically placed on the narrow Øresund strait that separates Denmark from Sweden. At the northern approach to Øresund lies Helsingør, better known in English as Elsinore, the setting for Shakespeare's tragedy *Hamlet, Prince of Denmark*.

Scandinavia's fun city

København – 'port of merchants' ... the Danish capital's very name makes clear its importance as a seaport and commercial centre. It is the largest city not only in Denmark – a quarter of the Danish population lives there

Visitors can enjoy every conceivable kind of entertainment at Tivoli, from the puppet theatre to the stand where, for a small sum, the henpecked husband can give vent to his frustrations by throwing wooden balls at an array of dishes ranged on a dresser. At night, multicoloured fairy lights and illuminated fountains lend an extra magic to the scene.

– but in the whole of Scandinavia. It is also generally regarded as the most lively city in Scandinavia.

Danes sometimes comment cheekily that even a Swede can enjoy himself in Copenhagen. And plenty of Swedes take the ferry or hydrofoil across the 12 miles of the Øresund strait to sample the city's delights, including those of alcohol that by Scandinavian standards is comparatively cheap.

One of the busiest parts of Copenhagen is the network of narrow, pedestrianised streets known as Strøget. These streets stretch north and east of Rådhuspladsen (Town Hall Square), and are like the Bond Street, Oxford Street and Covent Garden of Copenhagen. Here you will find all the smartest shops: the Royal Danish Porcelain shop, the premises of the famous Danish silversmith, Georg Jensen; and shops selling locally designed glassware, furniture and fabrics. Flourishing open-air cafés line the streets, and it is here that elegant shoppers and bejeaned students alike slump into the comfort of wicker chairs and watch the world go by. Kongens Nytorv Square lies at the north-eastern corner of Strøget. Here the Hotel d'Angleterre, the Royal Theatre, the Academy of Fine Arts and the French Embassy rub shoulders with the more earthy allure of neighbouring Nyhavn, until quite recently a popular haunt of sailors with its rough bars and tattoo shops, but now more renowned for its good restaurants.

To the south of the Town Hall Square stretches the astonishing Tivoli Gardens amusement park. The Gardens, which date from 1843, were the brainchild of the architect Georg Carstensen. He apparently persuaded King Christian VIII to let him lay them out by arguing that 'If only people are allowed to amuse themselves, they will forget to talk about politics'. People certainly amuse themselves in modern Tivoli. Its attractions include a concert hall, a pantomime theatre, bars, restaurants, fountains, fairy lights and seesaws.

Dutch architecture has had a strong influence on this city of brick walls and gleaming copper roofs and domes. As if to make up for the flatness of the country as a whole countless high spires and towers soar into the skies above Copenhagen. These range from the striking dragon-tail spire of the Dutch-style Børsen (Stock Exchange), through the gold and green pinnacle of Our Saviour's Church with its curious spiral staircase winding around it, to the looming early 20th-century tower of the Town Hall. Other outstanding monuments include Rosenborg Castle built in the early 17th century by King Christian IV, who was responsible for much of Copenhagen's architectural splendour; the Baroque Charlottenborg Castle, now the seat of the Art Academy; and the royal family's Amalienborg Palace.

Copenhagen is a city of fine food. Reigning supreme is *smørrebrød* – literally, 'bread and butter', but really an open sandwich. There are more than 200 different kinds of *smørrebrød* and they are all a joy to behold, with the pink of the prawns, say, set off by the saffron yellow of a sauce dotted with coriander. Anyone who has tried herring prepared in the Danish way will hardly want to taste it any other way; and the match between herring and the caraway-flavoured spirit, *akvavit,* is a Danish marriage that will never end in divorce.

According to the Danes, their national flag, the 'Dannebrog', is the oldest in Europe. They bring it out on any appropriate occasion, and in summer it flutters cheerfully from the flagpoles that stand in almost every country garden. In spring, students newly released from the rigours of their final exams brandish the flag with a mixture of relief and pride.

Iceland

Lost in the icy wilds of the North Atlantic, Iceland is none the less
an integral part of Europe. In the Middle Ages it boasted an epic
literature worthy of comparison with that of ancient Greece.
To this day Icelanders, who speak one of the oldest tongues in
Europe, have a passionate interest in books and learning. They are
also a down-to-earth people who have used modern technology to
harness the volcanic energy of their island and thereby offset the
rigours of its climate. The landscape is wild, harsh and beautiful,
almost lunar in places ... and it has so far escaped the worst
effects of pollution that afflict so much of mainland Europe.

The tiny toy-town port of Flateyri in the far north-west of Iceland is dwarfed by snow-patched mountains. Inhabitants of this remote community on the shores of Önundarfjördur enjoy a high standard of living gained from a hard life on the open seas.

This land of volcanoes set in a polar sea offers an unusual variety of swimming experiences, from a dip in the icy ocean, through a plunge into a hot pool, to a paddle along the steaming, snow-banked waters of a river near Reykjavík.

Previous page:
Icelanders, like all Nordics, love children. Yet it will not be long before these cheerful toddlers confront some of the responsibilities of adult life. Iceland's small population and its consequent shortage of manpower mean that teenagers can pick up lucrative summer work, although an ever-watchful State obliges them to save a proportion of their earnings.

Island of Fire and Ice

Just outside Iceland's capital of Reykjavík there rises a rocky mass where, according to local folklore, trolls – those unpleasantly vindictive creatures of Nordic mythology – are said to live. A few years ago the Icelandic Ministry of Transport proposed building a new road across these heights. The capital's six daily newspapers immediately set to, reminding their readers of the ancient legend. Then the general public took up the cry. What if the bulldozers started to break down for no apparent reason? What if workers on the site began to fall sick with illnesses that no one could explain? In the face of such an outcry the authorities climbed down and the new road was redirected to bypass the ill-omened site.

According to official statistics, Iceland's population is just over a quarter of a million, but this does not account for the trolls, elves and ghosts that seem so real to the local imagination. If the sceptical foreigner smiles, a local will take him to the French Embassy building in Reykjavík. In 1936, the French explorer Jean Charcot spent his last night there before embarking on his ship with the endearing name *Pourquoi-pas?* Soon after setting out, the ship sank with all hands. Since then, as many in Reykjavík will tell you, Charcot's spirit has stalked the Embassy's corridors.

It is somewhat surprising that a nation which has distinguished itself by its hard-headed application of modern technology to the exploitation of the island's natural resources should have this curious streak of superstition. And yet this paradox perhaps reflects part of the secret of the Icelanders' success. The inhabitants of this extraordinary island of volcanic fire and polar ice have harnessed imaginative flair on the one hand and down-to-earth common sense on the other, to the very concrete pursuit of an improved standard of living in the modern world.

Volcanoes and boiling springs

Iceland is almost entirely volcanic. Its eastern and western parts are mainly composed of volcanic basalt, and this covers roughly half the surface of the island. Since Iceland was first settled permanently by the Norwegian chieftain Ingólfur Arnarson in AD 874, some 150 volcanoes have become active. Over the last

few centuries, the island has seen, on average, one volcanic eruption every five years. If the products such as pumice that are obtained from lava were as valuable as oil, Iceland would be extremely rich: over the course of the last 500 years, a third of the world's lava has been produced by Icelandic volcanoes.

Icelanders can claim to be the world's most expert 'volcanic firemen'. In the early hours of January 23, 1973, a volcano on Heimaey, the only inhabited island of the Vestmann group off the country's southern coast, erupted with savage violence, and continued to erupt for five months. The Icelandic authorities dealt with the crisis with extraordinary skill and ingenuity. Within a few hours of the initial eruption, Heimaey's entire population of 5300 people had been evacuated without loss of life. It was too late to save large parts of the town, which were already smothered in thick layers of volcanic ash, and over the following days and weeks molten lava began to flow down over some of the residential streets. However, the authorities were determined to protect the port area and some important

The Öræfajökull glacier in south-east Iceland has a curiously metallic sheen. Glaciers cover more than 11 per cent of the surface of the island and reach thicknesses of more than 3000 feet. The rivers fed by this glacier cross plains of gravel and sand known as sandar, *which cover large areas along the country's south coast.*

fish-processing plants. Using gigantic plastic pipes, they pumped thousands of tons of sea water out of the harbour and emptied it at certain key points in the lava flow. This lowered the temperature of the magma by some 360° F and created dykes of hardened lava that redirected the flow that was continuing to pour out of the volcano.

In Iceland the opposites of fire and water, heat and cold, boiling springs and sheets of ice, are never far apart. Bubbling *hverir* springs, where the water can reach temperatures of well over normal boiling point, are common in the volcanic zones of the east and west, and there are more than 700 of them in all. They provide three-quarters of Iceland's population with central heating. The Deildartunguhver spring in western Iceland is probably the largest hot spring in the world, spewing out some 55 gallons of water per second. The most famous of Iceland's geysers – hot springs that spout water high into the air like a fountain – is the Great Geyser in southern Iceland. It used to send up a jet as high as 250 feet but has recently been relatively inactive. At the same time, just over 11 per cent of the country is covered with icy glaciers. The largest glacier, Vatnajökull, is equal in area to all the glaciers on the European continent together; it extends for 3240 square miles and is over 3000 feet thick in places. The ice cover waxes and wanes, and its retreat over the last century has exposed the relics of farms which were covered in the Middle Ages.

Iceland is largely a plateau with an average height of 1640 feet above sea level, although a quarter of the country lies below 1000 feet. Öræfajökull, the highest summit, rises to 6952 feet. Valleys cleave the western zone and are the most fertile agricultural areas, although even they are suitable only for grazing and growing fodder and root crops.

Viking pirates and Europe's first parliament

Iceland can lay claim to many marvels. It is the only country to enlarge its territory since the Second World War without encroaching on that of another country. This happened on November 15, 1963, when an underwater eruption south of the Vestmann Islands pushed three new islands to the surface. Two of these sank back again, but one remains – Surtsey (its name comes from Surtur, chief of the fire giants in Scandinavian mythology), with an area of nearly a quarter of a square mile.

This peaceful expansion was achieved by a country which does not even possess an army. Iceland has not always been so pacific, however. Its first settlers were Vikings, most of whom arrived in successive waves between AD 874 and 930 in search of new land. It is believed that many were Norwegian chieftains fleeing the centralisation of power under King Harald Hárfagri ('the Fair') of Norway. Having escaped the despotism of the Norwegian monarch, they had no intention of submitting themselves to a new thraldom. They therefore set up a kind of early republic and in AD 930 founded the first national parliament in Europe, the Althing. It met at Thingvellir, 30 miles east of Reykjavík, in an open-air lakeside arena overshadowed by lava crags. It was no assembly of bandits: members had to leave their weapons behind when taking their seats, and all decisions were taken in common, and were strictly bound by law. Those who refused to submit lost their protection under law and were obliged to leave the country.

The centuries that followed were far from trouble-free. Along with Greenland, Iceland agreed voluntarily to union with the Norwegian kingdom in 1262, and in 1380, the government of Iceland passed to Denmark. As the centuries passed Iceland suffered from acute poverty and a number of severe natural disasters, famines and epidemics, and yet it managed to survive these blows with its personality intact.

Independence from Denmark came in a series of stages after 1874, but on June 17, 1944, while Iceland was occupied by Allied troops and Denmark by the Germans, Iceland took the opportunity to declare itself a fully independent republic.

Cars and a solitary pedestrian struggle through the snowbound streets of Reykjavík, while a gap between the houses reveals a glimpse of the sea. By the standards of the rest of Europe, the Icelandic capital is a modest place of 90,000 inhabitants. Yet it is no technological backwater. Icelanders are in the forefront of modern attempts to exploit and harness the forces of nature. Geothermal energy, for example, provides central heating for almost all the capital's homes.

Old language, new words

The Icelandic language evolved from the language spoken by settlers from western Norway in the 9th and 10th centuries. It has changed remarkably little over the centuries – at least in its written form. As a result, Icelanders of today do not experience that much difficulty in reading the old Icelandic sagas. Conversely, if – by some miracle – an Icelandic Viking who had died in around 1250 were to come back to modern Reykjavík and buy, say, the daily newspaper *Morgunbladid*, he would understand much of what he read, even if some of the events described left him rather puzzled.

That a Viking should be able to get the gist of an article dealing with the purchase of long-haul aeroplanes, for example, is extraordinary. The explanation is that Icelandic has used its own ancient root words – rather than those of Greek or Latin, as in most other European languages – to forge new words. This has been particularly true since the early 19th century when most of the words that Iceland had borrowed from other languages were replaced by purely Icelandic forms. So, for instance, the word for long-haul aeroplane is *millilandaflugvél* ('between-lands-flying-machine').

This fashionable young Icelander seems the epitome of modern European youth. And yet, beneath the surface of any Icelander, young or old, landsman or seaman, you will find a deeply romantic soul with an extraordinary devotion to Nature and to Iceland's ancient Viking traditions. In a country where the standard of education is among the highest in the world, belief in the powers – for good or for ill – of the ghosts and spirits of Nordic folklore remains deeply rooted.

If a country exists where the lure of television has yet to replace the joy of reading, then Iceland is it. Reykjavík alone has no fewer than six daily newspapers – that is, one paper for every 14,000 inhabitants. Icelanders also nourish a passion for poetry, and a popular volume of poetry may be bought by a tenth of the island's population when it is first published.

Similarly, a cinema film is *kvikmynd* ('living picture'), psychology *sálfrædi* ('soul knowledge'), and materialism *efnishyggja* ('matter thinking').

By contrast, a Danish, Swedish or Norwegian Viking who returned to his country of origin today would have only a very sketchy understanding of what his descendants were saying or writing. For these three continental Scandinavian languages have borrowed extensively from modern German, English and French, not to mention the numerous words which have come from ancient Greek or Latin.

The sagas – deeds of love and war

Iceland has a strong literary tradition. It is perhaps best known for its Viking sagas, prose epics which tell of the families and feuds of the early generations of settlers, who lived in Iceland from 930 to 1030. These tales of adventure are often interspersed with pieces of ancient verse and elements of fantasy, and give a picture of the lives and bloody deeds of the early Scandinavians. Among the most celebrated is *Egill's Saga*, probably

written around 1225 and perhaps the work of Snorri Sturluson. Snorri is also known as the author of *The Prose Edda*, a handbook for poets in which he retells the myths and legends of the ancient Germans as preserved in the lays of *The Poetic Edda*.

The saga is based on fact, although it has been embellished in the telling. It relates the story of one of the most famous warrior poets of an earlier generation, Egill, younger son of Skallagrimur (Grimur the Bald), who was also known as a skilled practitioner of the arts of medicine and magic.

Egill was an infant prodigy who, at the age of three, was composing poetry that astonished his elders. Later he led the roving life of a Viking pirate. He went to Sweden and then to England, joining the court of King Athelstan and fighting for the king at a battle often identified with the Battle Brunanburh in AD 937. According to the saga – though almost certainly incorrectly – it was here that Egill's revered elder brother Thorolfur met his death. After this, Egill married his brother's widow and took up his sword once more in a bitter family feud, which went back to his father's disputes with the Norwegian king Eiríkur Blódöx (Eric Blood-Axe). Egill fell into the hands of his royal enemy, by now King of York, and was condemned to death. The king pardoned him on hearing a flattering lay he had composed the night before he was due to be executed.

The saga preserves some of Egill's verse, including two beautiful elegies. One was composed in memory of his favourite son, Bodvar, who drowned at sea, and includes a eulogy on the virtues of poetry and its ability to snatch joy from the jaws of grief. The other was dedicated to his wise and faithful friend Arinbjörn, who had counselled him to compose the lay for King Eirikur that won him his pardon.

Fishing remains the principal economic activity in Iceland. Cod continues to reign supreme, but the country is also exploring other areas of the fish industry, and its trout and salmon, for example, rival those of Norway for quality. Needless to say, local consumption of fish is high.

The bundles of dried cod lining the quay at Húsavík on Iceland's north coast and the rows of moored fishing vessels are signs of the port's prosperity. Húsavík is one of the oldest places in Iceland and is an important centre for cod-fishing with a lively social scene. All the houses are heated geothermally from hot springs over ten miles away. The snow-clad mountains on the other side of the bay of Skjálfandi rise in the background.

The maroon and white church of Raufarhöfn stands on a green bank above the icy waters of Thistilfjördur. Raufarhöfn is Iceland's most northerly community, lying on the edge of a region of almost desert-like barrenness less than ten miles south of the Arctic Circle.

A nation of bookworms

Icelanders buy and read an average of nine books per head of the population every year – a world record. It is hardly surprising, then, that Reykjavík is full of bookshops; that the publishers of a volume of poetry may hope to sell copies to a tenth of the population; or that the writer Halldór Laxness, winner of the Nobel Prize for Literature in 1955, enjoys the sort of popularity that in most countries would be accorded to a football hero.

Icelanders are exceptionally proud of their ancient culture and very sensitive to any threat to its integrity. The United States military base at Keflavík near the island's south-westernmost tip, is seen by many Icelanders as a symbol of American imperialism, and is a periodic target for political demonstrations. Before acceding to the highest office in the land, the current President, Vigdís Finnbogadóttir, was a keen supporter of this type of activity.

The President certainly shares the Icelanders' passion for their nation's culture. 'Our castles are literary,' she says. 'They are our legends and our epics.' President Vigdís was educated partly in France, and before her election was an enthusiastic tourist guide, showing the delights of her country to visiting parties of journalists and writers. She was also at various times teacher of French, a television producer, theatre director and member of an experimental theatre group in Reykjavík. Note that like most other Icelanders she does not have a surname in the normal sense of the word. People are always addressed by their first name. The second name, Icelanders say, is not a name but a fact – the first name of their father (or sometimes mother) followed by the suffix -son for men and -dottir for women. Thus Finnbogadóttir means 'daughter of Finnbogi'.

Iceland has, and has had, some curious laws. From 1924 until recently the people of Reykjavík were not

The Stokkur geyser erupts every two minutes, belching clouds of steam up to 70 ft (22m) into the air.

permitted to keep dogs in the city. This restriction, which was designed to avoid unnecessary noise and pollution in the capital, caused some opposition within the government. Albert Gudmundsson, a former Finance Minister, kept a dog hidden in his Reykjavík flat until a neighbour saw him out walking the animal one night and reported him to the authorities. Requested to pay a fine roughly equivalent to £200, the minister reckoned that tax revenue was already quite high enough and refused to pay up, despite a lawsuit brought against him by the city authorities. At one point he threatened to resign and seek exile in France, where he had once lived as a professional footballer. In the end, however, the minister kept his dog and eventually the law was changed to allow dogs in Reykjavík.

Iceland vs Britain: the Cod War

Iceland has always lived off its fishing industry, which still accounts for more than 70 per cent of its exports, although employing only 7.5 per cent of the work force. It was the importance of this resource that led the country into the Cod War with the United Kingdom.

In 1972 Iceland unilaterally extended its territorial waters from 12 to 50 miles, and in 1975 still farther to 200 nautical miles. These were controversial moves, designed to protect fish stocks around Iceland from overfishing by British, German, Soviet and French trawlermen. The International Court of Justice in The Hague refused to ratify the measure, but it did agree to limit the quotas of fish that foreign fishermen were allowed to catch in the area.

British trawlermen, however, decided to ignore the Icelanders' move, and a confrontation – with distinct

A geothermal power plant rises behind the warm waters of a blue lagoon which are believed to cure skin complaints. Iceland derives around a third of its energy from the exploitation of geothermal power.

One of Iceland's 150 active volcanoes flares behind a village cemetery. At least one of the island's volcanoes erupts every five years.

touches of farce about it – soon developed. British and Icelandic trawlermen hurled abuse and even fish entrails at each other from their boats. The Icelandic coastguard also started cutting the wire of the British boats' nets with enormous scissors. The situation continued to deteriorate with one of Iceland's three coastguard vessels firing on the British trawler *Everton*. At about the same time, 2000 Icelandic demonstrators stormed the British Embassy in Reykjavík and ransacked it. The British Government, under pressure from its own fishing industry, sent in the Royal Navy to try to protect its trawlers.

In this conflict of David against Goliath, the most embarrassed onlooker was the United States. Iceland has no armed forces but is none the less a member of NATO – a particularly important member during the Cold War in view of its key strategic position in the North Atlantic. Under an agreement dating from 1941,

the United States is responsible for defending the country. The American Government thus found itself in an awkward diplomatic position between two important allies. To make matters worse, the Soviet Union began to show a suspicious interest in the whole affair. The international interest worked in Iceland's favour, however. Iceland managed to win substantial concessions and its fertile seas remained protected.

Budgetary juggling

Like other Scandinavian countries, Iceland enjoys a comprehensive and efficient social welfare system, with individual poverty a rarity – although even at the beginning of the century, this was far from being the case.

For all that, its economy has proved fragile at times.

A day at the market. Iceland's million or so sheep roam across large parts of the island. Their wool is spun locally and used to make clothes and carpets which are exported to the United States and Russia.

In Iceland, as in Norway, turf is often used to cover the roofs of barns and stables. Arable agriculture is negligible here – only 1 per cent of the land is cultivated. Instead, the Icelandic smallholder raises livestock.

Inflation has been a constant problem; in 1983 it reached a high point of over 84 per cent. Governments since then have managed to bring it down considerably, so that in 1989 inflation was running at 22.3 per cent. And the early 1990s have seen a stabilisation of the economy with inflation down to between 5 and 7 per cent and interest rates between 8.5 and 10 per cent.

One consequence of all this has been a flexible social structure. Interest rates remain reasonably high, but a small work force means that unemployment is almost non-existent. As a result, a university lecturer, for example, might do a few hours' extra work a week at a fish-processing plant to help to meet his monthly mortgage repayments and even the President herself held several jobs, sometimes simultaneously, before reaching her present office. Another aspect of this flexibility is that people frequently move from a job in one field to another in a quite different field without any apparent difficulty. Even children have plenty of opportunities. Teenagers have been known to earn more than £2000 a month on the boats during their four-month summer holiday. But they do not get to spend it all: the government has set up a system of compulsory savings for a proportion of their income.

Polar bananas – greenhouse miracles

Today, only about 30 per cent of the energy consumed in Iceland is generated from imported oil, and this figure is declining all the time. Hydroelectricity accounts for a further 37 per cent, and 30 per cent comes from the exploitation of geothermal power – that

Towering crags loom over farm buildings spread out across a flat valley bottom. Most Icelandic farms lie in remote valleys or on the isolated shores of distant fjords. Just over 20 per cent of the island's surface consists of grazing land such as this. A few enterprising farms have tapped the power of thermal springs to heat acres of greenhouses for growing tomatoes, cucumbers and even bananas.

is, by tapping the energy potential of hot springs. Geothermal energy is becoming increasingly important, since Iceland currently exploits only one-tenth of its potential from this source.

Geothermal energy has been used chiefly for heating homes. In 1989, over 80 per cent of Iceland's population lived in geothermally heated homes. Hot water direct from the springs (in Reykjavík some lie within the boundaries of the city itself) is mixed with cooler water that has already been through a town or village's central heating systems and been fed back into the system. This can be achieved for just 40 per cent of the cost of fossil-fuel heating. A number of market gardeners have also taken advantage of this exceptionally cheap form of energy to heat their greenhouses, so that within 100 miles of the Arctic Circle they have succeeded in growing tomatoes, cucumbers, flowers and even bananas.

Industry, too, has started to harness geothermal energy to its needs, with some success. At Bjarnarflag, by Lake Myvatn in the north-east, geothermal energy is used to process diatomite – a kind of finely powdered earth widely used as a filtering agent and insulator – extracted from the lake bed. A factory in the north-west uses geothermal energy in the processing of kelp, and, on a larger scale, an experimental power station has been built at Krafla, a mountain peak in the north-east, to produce electricity geothermally. Here, however, volcanic eruptions and frequent earthquakes pose a constant threat to the work, and will have to be overcome before Iceland can fully exploit its geothermal potential.

Home sweet home

At the beginning of the 20th century, Iceland was an agricultural country depending heavily on grazing and livestock farming. Although these are no longer so important to the economy, Iceland continues to profit from its livestock. The Icelandic pony, once the island's chief draught animal, has become popular among young riders in the United States and is widely exported. In addition, wool from the country's many sheep is made into carpets and clothes which are then exported to both the United States and Russia. The excellent local waters produce salmon and trout to rival those of Norway for quality, and the recent introduction of fish farms has met with some success.

Further proof of the Icelanders' commercial flair can be seen in the field of air transport. The State airline Flugleidir offers regular low-cost transatlantic flights with a stop-over in Iceland. The service compares favourably with those of the larger airlines.

The lure of abroad exercises an ever greater pull on the increasingly prosperous Icelanders during the holiday months. The harshness of the island's climate, the country's geographical isolation and also, strangely, the very friendliness of a society where privacy is at a premium – all these combine to send droves of Icelanders south in summer. For a few weeks they enjoy sweltering heat, cheap wine and beer and all the delights which are hard to come by at home. And yet for most of them, it is with pleasure that, at the end of their holidays, they board the plane home, bound for their near-Arctic island.

The shaggy-maned Iceland pony can be seen all over the island, roaming wild and grazing by the sides of roads and on mountain slopes. Despite its diminutive size, it is a sturdy beast which was used to pull ploughs and carts before the arrival of the tractor and motor car.

The traditional fittings of an Icelandic interior: a row of panelled beds down one side of the room, spinning wheels, and in the far room a painted trunk. Icelandic furniture, like that of the other Nordic countries, is plain but has an austere elegance of its own.

Greenland

This cold island of the Arctic north may be green in parts during
the summer, but for the long winter months it is a place of ice and
snow. Here, for many centuries, the Inuit, or Eskimos, have hunted
and fished, carving a hard living from a hostile environment.
Here, too, adventurers, from Vikings to the 20th-century polar
explorers, have sought new fields to conquer. Then came the shock
of the new. During the last four decades, the world's largest island
has experienced dramatic change, bringing it firmly into the
modern world.

Preceding page:
Two young Greenland girls are dressed in traditional finery that is both colourful and snug. The ancestors of the Inuit (Greenlanders have little affection for the term Eskimo, which means 'eater of raw flesh') originally came from Asia. They made their way across the Bering Strait, then overland to what is now northern Canada and on into Greenland.

At one point it was suggested that Greenland should become an exporter of water. Saudi Arabia and the emirates of the Arabian Gulf were studying an intriguing solution to their water problem: towing icebergs to the Middle East.

Green Land or White Land?

Greenland's Viking discoverer, Eirik the Red, would undoubtedly have fallen foul of any official, 10th-century body concerned with advertising standards. When he gave the name of Greenland to the greyish-white land he had discovered to the west of Iceland, Eirik was being distinctly misleading. A Norwegian by birth, who settled in Iceland in his late teens, Eirik had been banished from Iceland after committing a murder, but he then returned home in the hope of recruiting a few adventurous souls to join him in colonising his new-found land. As a good publicity man, he knew he had to make the place sound enticing. And so he had no qualms in painting a shamelessly rosy picture of it.

Yet his deception was only partial. In southern Greenland, which is on roughly the same latitude as the region around Oslo in Norway, a few brilliantly green valleys scoop their way inland during the brief summer. There are even a handful of stunted birch trees that somehow manage to cling on to life.

This green fringe is negligible, however, when compared with the huge ice cap that permanently covers more than three-quarters of the world's largest island. Greenland's ice cap is the largest glaciated mass outside of Antarctica, extending for 839,550 square miles, some three times the area of Texas. It reaches a depth of 9840 feet in the east and rises to just under 10,600 feet above sea level at its highest point. It has been estimated that if as a result of global warming this giant ice cube melted, the world's oceans would rise by 23 feet. As it is, blocks of ice, or 'snouts', regularly break off from the ice cap where it touches the sea, to form icebergs.

'The Seal of God'

When Eirik the Red, with his companions, horses, sheep and goats, eventually came ashore in the fjords of southern Greenland in AD 986, the island was uninhabited. Not long after the Vikings had settled,

Modern Inuit live in houses of wood and stone and are surrounded by all the paraphernalia of the Western lifestyle. Their children go to schools where they are taught in Danish and the Inuit language known as Greenlandic, and study all the usual academic subjects. They do not quite lose touch with their roots, however – they also learn how to paddle a kayak and throw a harpoon.

Traditionally, the Inuit hunted whales in kayaks. But that old form of man-to-beast combat has long since died out. Modern methods of finding and capturing whales have led to a reduction in the world whale population from 5 million to less than 1 million, and some species are now threatened with extinction.

Greenlanders are a mixture of Inuit and European blood. People of pure Inuit blood nowadays live only in the far north and in east Greenland. Whatever their ethnic origins, Greenlanders enjoy the benefits of the 'consumer society', whose products are readily available in immense supermarkets.

Greenland passed to Denmark. Greenland's climate began to deteriorate slowly from about 1350, and conditions for farming grew less favourable. The ships that supplied the Norse settlers dwindled and then ceased altogether; and by about 1500 the descendants of Eirik the Red and his fellows had become extinct, leaving Greenland to the Inuit.

European cartographers and geographers continued to remember Greenland through all these centuries, but it figured in their imaginations purely as a fantastic place of legend and saga. Only in the late 16th century was it rediscovered by English explorers including Martin Frobisher (1576-7) and John Davis (1585). This heralded a new era in Greenland's history. European whalers began to ply the waters of the warmer western coast, lured by the profits to be gained from whale oil, a valuable commodity chiefly used in lamps. The Inuit, meanwhile, looked on in astonishment. Some 10,000 Europeans – particularly Dutch – caught as many as 1000 whales a year off Greenland's coasts.

The Danes, who along with Norway still theoretically ruled Greenland, then decided that the activities of the Dutch seamen ran counter to their own interests. In 1721 the Norwegian missionary Hans Egede established a colony at Godthåb (or Nuuk, in the language of the Inuit), the modern capital of Greenland. Egede also set about converting the Inuit to Christianity, a task that required some ingenuity. To make himself understood he had to adapt many of the most familiar Christian prayers and images: 'Give us this day our daily bread'

In Greenland's capital, Godthåb (or Nuuk, in Greenlandic), fresh cod can be bought direct from the fishermen. Cod is a favourite dish during the brief summer. Otherwise, the local cuisine relies heavily on seal and reindeer meat. Greenlanders also make a pudding that looks rather like plum pudding from seal fat and bilberries.

however, a quite different group of invaders – the Inuit (Eskimos) – began to arrive by kayak from the north of what is now Canada, and started to establish themselves on Greenland's north-eastern shores.

The two cultures lived side by side for several centuries, warring occasionally, but mostly maintaining a reasonable understanding with each other. In the end, however, it was the Inuit who survived the longest. In 1261 Greenland came under the official sovereignty of the Norwegian crown, but in 1397 the government of

became 'Give us this day our daily meat', and 'the Lamb of God' became 'the Seal of God', for the Inuit knew nothing of either bread or lambs. More colonies were founded along the west coast but there was no large-scale development. It became a fundamental principle of Danish colonial policy that Greenland should stay isolated – partly to protect the Inuit. As a result, the Inuits' traditional way of life – fishing and hunting seals, whales, polar bears and the few birds that reached their island – continued unmolested well into the 20th century.

The shock of the new

In 1953 life began to change for Greenland's Inuit. For this was the year in which Greenland's status changed from being a colony to being an integral part of the Kingdom of Denmark. The Greenlanders were given the right to send two elected representatives to the Folketing (Parliament) in Copenhagen. A commission was set up, with members from both Denmark and Greenland, and this embarked on an ambitious building and modernisation programme.

Thousands of Danish workers descended on the small communities of western Greenland, dynamiting and flattening their way across large areas of ground, constructing hospitals, schools, blocks of flats, power stations, roads, ports and factories. Another objective of

the authorities was to eliminate tuberculosis, which had long been endemic in Greenland. After ten years, the illness was eradicated, and living conditions had generally improved beyond recognition. Next it was the turn of education. In the early 1960s, Greenland's schools were completely reorganised, and many hundreds of young Greenlanders were sent to Denmark to further their studies. A new generation grew up with attitudes and expectations that were quite different from those of their parents.

Developments continued, as Greenlanders came to feel more strongly about their cultural and political integrity. In 1979 Greenland won home rule, but it remained a nominal part of Denmark. And then, in 1985, it quit the European Community – the first nation to do so since the EC's foundation. 'We just don't

The fishing port of Narssaq (the 'Plain') lies on Greenland's southern tip. During the coldest months of winter, its fishing fleet is icebound. Its 1600 inhabitants then occupy themselves in other ways. There are seal and fish-processing plants and two canning factories, one for fish, the other for shelled prawns.

Summer in Narssaq presents a very different scene, with mini-icebergs bobbing in the bright blue waters of the fjord. This is the time for the cod harvest. Some 1000 tons of cod, either sun-dried or deep-frozen, are dispatched each year to the United States and Europe, and cod roe is a growing export product.

belong to Europe', commented one of the key advocates of this move, Greenland's concertina-playing prime minister, the Lutheran pastor Jonathan Motzfeldt. 'We are a polar people. Our ties are with the Inuit of Canada, Alaska and Siberia. We want to make our own future.'

Motzfeldt and his colleagues are confident that they will make their own future. Certainly, the Greenland of the 1990s is very different from what it was just 40 years ago. Fishing continues to be one of its people's chief occupations, but now it operates on an industrial scale with cod and shrimp the major part of the catch. The country is also rich in mineral resources: it exports lead and zinc from a mine near Uummannaq on the north-western coast; it has untapped reserves of uranium in the south; and some oil companies believe there may be oil reserves beneath the eastern coast. Greenland also benefits economically from two American bases in the west of the country.

There is also now a growing tourist trade. Holidaymakers are flown by helicopter (roads are still few, despite the earlier work of the Danish authorities) to villages along the west coast, where the many attractions include sea-fishing and exploring the fringes of the still empty interior on foot and sledge. At the same time, hunting still remains an important livelihood for many Greenlanders.

Winter fishermen bore holes in the ice to catch crabs and fish in the waters below. To reach their prey they often have to drop lines several hundreds of yards long.

A pair of huskies gambol in the snow at Kulusuk on Greenland's eastern coast. Until recently, Kulusuk was cut off for over nine months each year, since only at the beginning of July does the ice melt sufficiently to allow boats to enter its harbour.

The construction of a United States radar station has changed many of the old patterns of life, however. Even so, the motorised skidoo has still not replaced the traditional sledge in the affections or lives of the local inhabitants.

Nowadays no one in Greenland lives in igloos except during long winter hikes. The igloo is, however, a highly practical dwelling, offering effective protection against storms. A traditional igloo is about as high as a man and its diameter should be roughly equal to two ski sticks. It takes three people with shovels and ice cutters less than two hours to build. Even in the extreme cold, the temperature inside never sinks below zero.

Brigitte Bardot and the seal-hunters

The French beauty and animal-rights activist Brigitte Bardot may once have fired the hearts of many men – but not those of Nuusuaq, a village on Greenland's west coast. Its 140 inhabitants make their living from seal-hunting and object to her campaign against the hunting of seal pups. As a result of the boycotts organised by Ms Bardot and her colleagues, there has been a dramatic, worldwide collapse in the price of sealskin. The villagers of Nuusuaq, whose livelihoods have been damaged, feel that they are the victims of a misunderstanding, for it is in Canada, not in Greenland, they insist, that seal pups, rather than adult seals, are hunted to death. They also emphasise that Greenlanders were taking steps to protect their animal life long before environmental organisations appeared on the scene.

As seal hunting still plays a comparatively important part in Greenland's economy – until recently, about a fifth of the population earned its livelihood from sealing – it is hardly surprising that local hunters get very indignant at the bad press they so often receive around the world. They have suffered, too, as a result of a recommendation by the European Parliament that the import of the pelts of young seals should be banned. Although the measure does not directly affect Greenland's sealers, since they only slaughter adult seals, it has none the less encouraged a further decline in the price of sealskin.

Modern times

The sealers are among the last Greenlanders whose way of life resembles that of their forebears. Increasingly, the rest of their countrymen are being drawn to the towns, lured by the prospect of secure jobs such as those in the fish factories. Godthåb, with a population of 10,500 – about the size of a small British town – is now home to nearly one fifth of Greenland's inhabitants. Families which would once have wandered the ice as nomadic hunters with harpoons, kayaks, huskies and rifles, now get their food from supermarkets.

The abandonment of traditional patterns of life has not been painless. Early travellers to Greenland commented on an unusual aspect of Inuit hospitality whereby, when entertaining visitors, Inuit men would lend them their wives. In return, the visitors were expected to make a small gift, a packet of needles, say. Obviously, customs have changed, but the tradition of sexual freedom remains. Greenland also has the highest suicide rate in the world, about one per thousand.

In less than one generation, the Greenlanders have moved from the primitive to the modern. It is a remarkable achievement, even if, as in so many countries around the world, the 'blessings' of a Western way of life have often proved double-edged. Still, the Inuit are a resilient race – as their survival for so many centuries in such hostile environments has shown. No doubt, as Pastor Motzfeldt hopes, they will prove themselves capable of forging their own future.

Unlike the Lapps of Scandinavia, who use reindeer, the Inuit rely on their dogs to pull their sledges. Indeed, their whole way of life is quite different from that of the Lapps. Where the Lapps are herdsmen, the Inuit are hunters, traditionally of polar bears and seals. Nowadays, the Innuit do most of their hunting in the north, which has always been the main preserve of the polar bear. Recent climatic warming has also resulted in seals abandoning more southerly waters for the colder waters of the north.

Gazetteer

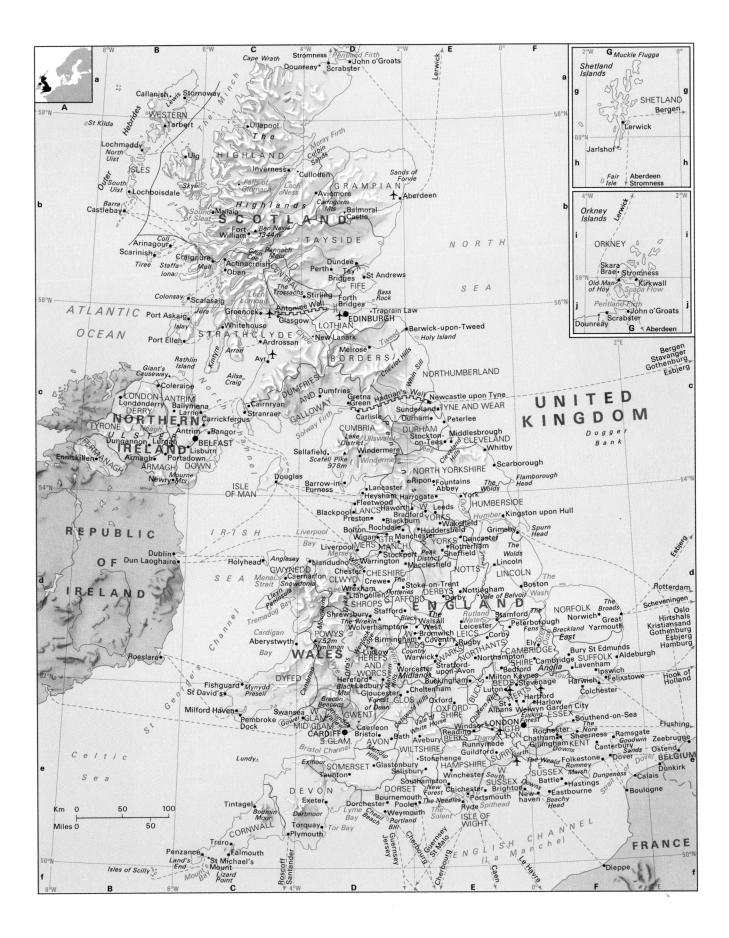

THE UNITED KINGDOM AT A GLANCE

Area 94,225 square miles

Terrain Rugged hills and low mountains to north and west, plains and rolling hills towards south and east

Population 57,366,000

Population density 609 people per square mile

Capital London

Government Parliamentary monarchy

Currency Pound sterling = 100 pence

Languages English, Gaelic, Welsh

Ethnic divisions 81.5% English, 9.6% Scottish, 4.2% Irish, 1.9% Welsh, 2.8% West Indian, Indian, Pakistani and other

Religions Christian (55% Protestant, 10% Roman Catholic), Muslim (2%), Jewish, Hindu and Sikh minorities

Climate Temperate; average London temperatures range from 4.5°C (40°F) in January to 18°C (64°F) in July. Average rainfall 24 inches (600mm)

Main primary products Wheat, barley, potatoes, sugar beet, fruit and vegetables, fish; oil and natural gas, coal

Major industries Agriculture, oil and gas extraction and refining, coal mining, machinery and transport equipment, iron and steel, metals, food processing, paper and paper products, textiles, chemicals, clothing, light industry, finance and business services

Main exports Agricultural and industrial machinery, crude oil and petroleum products, chemicals, transport equipment, vehicles, aircraft, electrical goods, iron and steel, nonferrous metals, textiles, food products

Transport Rail 10,307 miles standard gauge; Public Roads 217,789 miles (surfaced 217,789 miles); Airports 379

Government expenditure (US$) 328 billion (defence 35 billion)

Annual income per head (US$) 7550

Armed services 306,000

International affiliations NATO; British Commonwealth; OECD; EC

Literacy 99%

Full-time students 334,000

Population growth (per thous/yr) 3

Fertility 1.8 children born per woman

Marriage rate (per 1000 people) 13.9

Divorce rate (per 1000 people) 6.4

Life expectancy (yrs) Male 73 **Female** 79

IRELAND AT A GLANCE

Area 27,136 square miles

Terrain Mostly level to rolling interior plain surrounded by rugged hills and low mountains, sea cliffs on west coast

Population 3,500,000

Population density 129 people per square mile

Capital Dublin

Government Parliamentary republic

Currency Punt = 100 pighne

Languages English, Irish

Ethnic divisions Celtic with English minority

Religion Christian (91% Roman Catholic, 3% Church of Ireland, 1% Presbyterian)

Climate Temperate, warmed by the North Atlantic Drift. Average temperatures range from 4-7°C (39-45°F) in January/February to 14-16°C (57-61°F) in July/August

Main primary products Cereals, potatoes, sugar beet, vegetables, livestock, fish; peat, natural gas, lead, zinc, barytes, gypsum

Major industries Agriculture, food processing, machinery, chemicals and fertilisers, textiles, clothing, tourism

Main exports Machinery, chemicals, meat, dairy produce, textile yarns and fabrics, instruments, livestock

Transport Rail 1208 miles 5ft 3in gauge; Public Roads 57,357 miles (surfaced 57,357 miles); Airports 37

Government expenditure (US$) 11.2 billion (defence 500 million)

Annual income per head (US$) 8500

Armed services 13,000

International affiliations OECD; EC

Literacy 99%

Full-time students 66,350

Population growth (per thous/yr) -4

Fertility 2.1 children born per woman

Marriage rate (per 1000 people) 5.1

Divorce rate (per 1000 people) no legal procedure for divorce

Life expectancy (yrs) Male 72 **Female** 78

NORWAY AT A GLANCE

Area 125,180 square miles

Terrain Glaciated, mostly high plateaus and rugged mountains broken by fertile valleys, small scattered plains; coastline deeply indented by fjords; arctic tundra in north

Population 4,253,000

Population density 34 people per square mile

Capital Oslo

Government Parliamentary monarchy

Currency Krone = 100 ore

Languages Norwegian (old - Riksmal, new - Landsmal), Lappish and Finnish

Ethnic divisions Minority of 20,000 Lapps

Religion Christian (88% Evangelical Lutheran, 1% Pentecostal)

Climate Temperate; cold in the north. Average temperature in Oslo ranges from -7 to -2°C (19-28°F) in January to 13-22°C (55-72°F) in July

Main primary products Barley, oats, potatoes, livestock, apples, timber, fish; crude oil and natural gas, coal, iron, lead, zinc, copper, nickel, titanium, quartz (silicon)

Major industries Mining, crude oil and natural gas refining, mineral refining, chemicals, shipbuilding, food processing, fishing, forestry, timber products

Main exports Crude oil and natural gas, aluminium and other nonferrous metals, chemicals, ships, machinery, fish, petroleum products, iron and steel, paper, timber products

Transport Rail 2523 miles standard gauge; Public Roads 54,791 miles (surfaced 37,922 miles); Airports 104

Government expenditure (US$) 41.3 billion (defence 2.5 billion)

Annual income per head (US$) 20,020

Armed services 36,800

International affiliations NATO, EFTA, OECD

Literacy 100%

Full-time students 57,300

Population growth (per thous/yr) 5

Fertility 1.8 children born per woman

Marriage rate (per 1000 people) 5.1

Divorce rate (per 1000 people) 2.2

Life expectancy (yrs) Male 73 **Female** 81

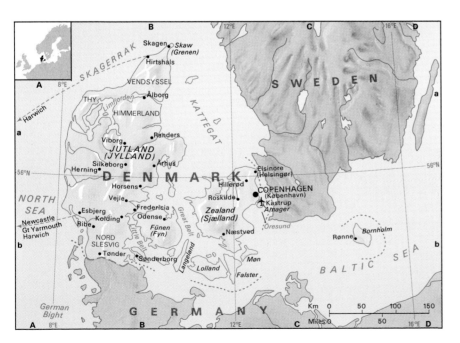

DENMARK AT A GLANCE

Area 16,629 square miles

Terrain Low and flat to gently rolling plains, a peninsula and over 480 islands

Population 5,131,000

Population density 309 people per square mile

Capital Copenhagen

Government Constitutional monarchy

Currency Krone = 100 ore

Language Danish

Ethnic divisions Scandinavian, Eskimo, Faroese, German

Religion Christian (Evangelical Lutheran)

Climate Temperate maritime; average temperature in Copenhagen: -3 to 2°C (27-36°F) in February; 14-22°C (57-72°F) in July

Main primary products Cattle, pigs, poultry, cereals, potatoes and other root crops, fodder, fish; some oil and natural gas

Major industries Agriculture, food processing, fishing, engineering, ship-building, petroleum refining, chemicals, furniture, leather

Transport Rail 1764 miles standard gauge; Public Roads 43,980 miles (surfaced 43,980 miles); Airports 114

Government expenditure (US$) 34 billion (defence 1.5 billion)

Annual income per head (US$) 18,470

Armed services 33,200

International affiliations NATO, EC, OECD

Literacy 99 %

Full-time students 101,500

Population growth (per thous/yr) 1

Fertility 1.6 children born per woman

Marriage rate (per 1000 people) 6.2

Divorce rate (per 1000 people) 2.9

Life expectancy (yrs) Male 73 **Female** 79

SWEDEN AT A GLANCE

Area 173,665 square miles

Terrain Mostly flat or gently rolling lowlands, mountains in west

Population 8,527,000

Population density 49 people per square mile

Capital Stockholm

Government Parliamentary monarchy

Currency Krona = 100 ore

Language Swedish

Ethnic divisions Homogeneous white population with small Lapp minority; about 12% foreign born or first-generation immigrants (Finns, Yugoslavs, Danes, Norwegians, Greeks, Turks)

Religion Christian (94% Evangelical Lutheran)

Climate Cool temperate with short, hot summers and long, cold winters. Average temperature in Stockholm ranges from -5 to -1°C (23-30°F) in February to 14-22°C (57-72°F) in July

Main primary products Dairy products, cereals, potatoes, sugar beet, rapeseed, timber; iron ore, copper, lead, zinc

Major industries Engineering and electrical goods, timber, timber products including wood pulp and paper, furniture

Main exports Engineering and electrical goods, timber, timber products, paper and wood pulp, motor vehicles, chemicals, iron and steel, petroleum products

Transport Rail 7147 miles standard gauge; Public Roads 127,387 miles (surfaced 43,386 miles); Airports 256

Government expenditure (US$) 57.9 billion (defence 4.7 billion)

Annual income per head (US$) 15,700

Armed services 64,500

International affiliations OECD, EFTA, EC application

Literacy 99%

Full-time students 178,000

Population growth (per thous/yr) 5

Fertility 1.9 children born per woman

Marriage rate (per 1000 people) 5.2

Divorce rate (per 1000 people) 2.2

Life expectancy (yrs) Male 75 **Female** 81

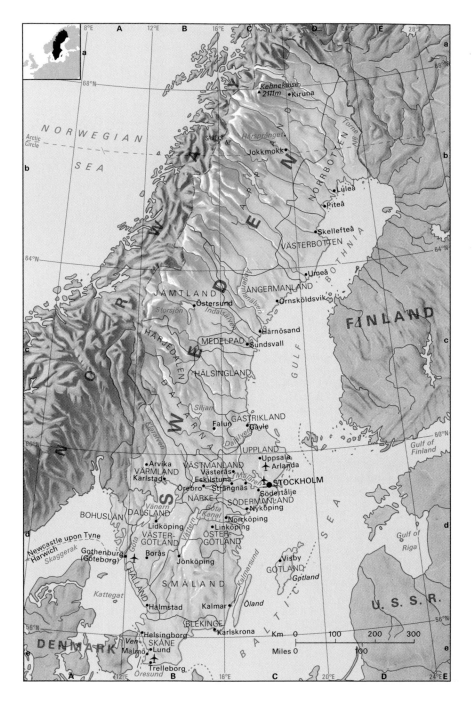

ICELAND AT A GLANCE

Area 39,768 square miles

Terrain Mostly plateau interspersed with mountain peaks, icefields; coast deeply indented by bays and fjords

Population 257,000

Population density 6 people per square mile

Capital Reykjavik

Government Parliamentary republic

Currency Krona = 100 aurar

Language Icelandic

Ethnic divisions Homogeneous mixture of descendants of Norwegians and Celts

Religion Christian (Evangelical Lutheran)

Climate Cold temperate; warmed by the North Atlantic Drift. Average temperature in Reykjavik ranges from -2 to 2°C (28-36°F) in January to 9-14°C (48-57°F) in July

Main primary products Fish, potatoes, sheep, dairy cattle, poultry

Major industries Fishing, fish and food processing, agriculture, cement, aluminium smelting

Main exports Fish, fish products, aluminium, wool and sheepskin products

Transport Rail none; Public Roads 7750 miles (surfaced 1429 miles); Airports 92

Government expenditure (US$) 1.7 billion (defence none)

Annual income per head (US$) 16,200

Armed services None

International affiliations OECD, EFTA

Literacy 100%

Full-time students 4700

Population growth (per thous/yr) 11

Fertility 2.2 children born per woman

Marriage rate (per 1000 people) 4.6

Divorce rate (per 1000 people) 2.1

Life expectancy (yrs) Male 75 **Female** 80

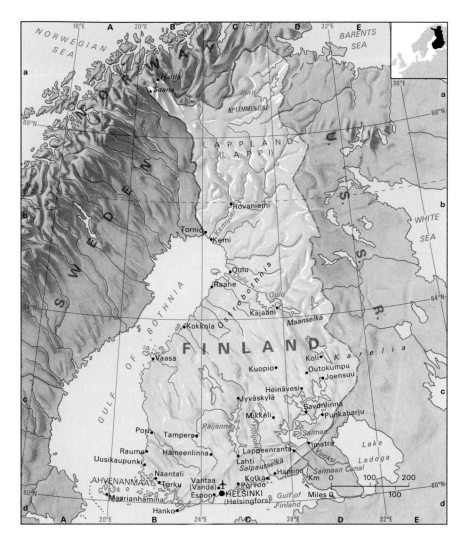

FINLAND AT A GLANCE
Area 130,557 square miles
Terrain Mostly low, flat to rolling plains interspersed with lakes and low hills
Population 4,977,000
Population density 38 people per square mile
Capital Helsinki
Government Parliamentary republic
Currency Markka = 100 penni
Languages Finnish, Swedish
Ethnic divisions Finn, Swede, Lapp, Gypsy, Tatar
Religion Christian (92% Lutheran, 1% Greek Orthodox)
Climate Temperate, with cold winters. Average temperature in Helsinki ranges from -9 to -4°C (16-25°F) in February to 12-22°C (54-72°F) in July
Main primary products Timber, cereals, potatoes, livestock, fish; copper, zinc, iron, chromium, lead
Major industries Forestry, timber products including wood pulp and paper, machinery, shipbuilding, clothing, chemicals, fertilisers
Main exports Paper, machinery, ships, timber, chemicals, clothing, wood pulp, petroleum products

Transport Rail 3643 miles 5ft gauge; Public Roads 48,008 miles (surfaced 28,394 miles); Airports 157
Government expenditure (US$) 28.1 billion (defence 1.4 billion)
Annual income per head (US$) 15,000
Armed services 35,200
International affiliations OECD; EFTA
Literacy Almost 100%
Full-time students 103,895
Population growth (per thous/yr) 3
Fertility 1.7 children born per woman
Marriage rate (per 1000 people) 5
Divorce rate (per 1000 people) 2.4
Life expectancy (yrs) Male 71 **Female** 80

GREENLAND AT A GLANCE
Area 840,000 square miles
Terrain Flat to gradually sloping icecap covers all but a narrow, mountainous, barren, rocky coast
Population 56,000
Population density 0.07 people per square mile
Capital Godthab (also known as Nuuk)
Government Self-governing part of Denmark
Currency Danish Krone = 100 ore
Languages Greenlandic (Eskimo) and Danish
Ethnic divisions 86% Greenlanders, 14% Danish
Religion Christian (Evangelical Lutheran)
Climate Polar; average temperature in the north (Thule) ranges from -23°C (-9°F) in February to 5°C (41°F) in July, and in the south from -8°C (18°F) to 10°C (50°F)
Main primary products Fish, sheep
Major industries Fishing, mining, fish and food processing, hides and skins

Main exports Fish and fish products, cryolite (used in making aluminium)
Government expenditure (US$) 380 million (defence none)
Annual income per head (US$) 9600
Defence employees None
International affiliations Self-governing overseas administrative division of Denmark
Literacy 99%
Full-time students 2300 in vocational training
Population growth (per thous/yr) 12
Fertility 2.2 children born per woman
Life expectancy (yrs) Male 62 **Female** 68

Picture Credits

p.7 Koch-Rapho; p.8 top Bernager-Explorer; bottom Stevens-Atlas-Photo; p.9 Bernager-Explorer; p.10 Andry Williams-Robert Harding Picture Library; p.11 left Gérard-A. Hutchison Lby; right Gérard-A. Hutchison Lby; p.12 Ribieras-Explorer; p.13 Hurn-Magnum; p.14 P. Ploquin; p.15 top Bernager-Explorer; bottom A. Hutchison Lby; p.16 P. Ploquin; p.17 P. Ploquin; p.18 Gérard-Explorer; p.19 Erath-Explorer; p.20 Boys-Rapho; p.21 Boys-Rapho; p.22 de Seynes-Rapho; p.23 C. Lénars; p.24 Patrix-Photothèque S.D.P.; p.25 bottom Seed-Rapho; p.26 Mazin-Top; p.27 Hartmann-Magnum; p.28 Rex Features; p.29 top Supp-Rapho; bottom Mazin-Top; p.30 Mazin-Top; p.31 top Seed-Rapho; bottom F. Peuriot; p.32 Gerry Cranham; p.33 Gérard-Explorer; p.34 top Ward-Ana; bottom Seed-Rapho; p.35 Spiegel-Rapho; p.36 P. Ploquin; p.37 Ward-Ana; p.38 Tétrel-Explorer; p.40 top Gérard-Explorer; bottom P. Ploquin; p.41 Roy-Explorer; p.42 Sioen-Cedri; p.43 Downman-A. Hutchison Lby; p.44 Rigal-Explorer; p.45 Joyce-Atlas-Photo; p.46 McBride-A.Hutchison Lby; p.47 Girard-Rapho; p.48 Gloaguen-Rapho; p.49 Quéméré-Cedri; p.50 Vautier-De Nanxe; p.51 Ducange-Top; p.52 Sioen-Cedri; p.53 top Seed-Rapho; bottom Serraillier-Rapho; p.54 top Petit-Top; bottom Petit-Top; p.55 Quéméré-Cedri; p.56 left Quéméré-Cedri; right Serraillier-Rapho; p.57 Ducange-Top; p.58 Desjardins-Top; p.59 left Desjardins-Top; right Poinot-Pix; p.60 Gerster-Rapho; p.61 Pinsard-Cedri; p.62 left Petit-Top; right F. Peuriot; p.63 Roy-Explorer; p.64 top Quémère-Cedri; bottom Roy-Explorer; p.65 Petit-Top; p.66 Serraillier-Rapho; p.67 Quéméré-Cedri; p.68 top Duncan Maxwell-Robert Harding Picture Library; bottom Quéméré-Cedri; p.69 Robert Harding Picture Library; p.70 top

Quéméré-Cedri; bottom Quéméré-Cedri; p.71 Pratt-Pries-Diaf; p.72 top Quéméré-Cedri; bottom Belzeaux-Rapho; p.73 de Laubier-Pix; p.74 Bouiillot-Marco Polo; p.75 Arnold-Magnum; p.76 Pratt-Pries-Diaf; p.77 top S.Held; bottom Kosossey-Leda; p.78 Serraillier-Rapho; p.79 Serraillier-Rapho; p.80 Berry-Magnum; p.81 left Poinot-Pix; right Boourbotte-Fotogram; p.82 Tetrel-Explorer; p.83 Quéméré-Cedri; p.84 Serraillier-Rapho; p.85 top Vandystadt; bottom de Laubier-Pix; p.86 Rousseau-Top; p.87 Uzan-Gamma; p.88 top M.Garanger; bottom Blouin-Diaf; p.89 Hurn-Magnum; p.90 C. Lénars; p.91 top Freed-Magnum; bottom Freed-Magnum; p.92 Gruyaert-Magnum; p.93 Gruyaert-Magnum; p.94 left Uzan-Gamma; right M. Guillard-Scope; p.95 Marquis-Explorer; p.96 Cagatay-Gamma; p.97 J. Guillard-Scope; p.98 M. Guillard-Scope; p.99 top Roy-Explorer; bottom Hurn-Magnum; p.100 J. Guillard-Scope; p.100/101 J. Guillard-Scope; p.101 Hurn Magnum; p.102 top M. Guillard-Scope; bottom D. Blouin; p.103 Rainon-Explorer; p.104 Freed-Magnum; p.105 Roy-Explorer; p.106 Gaumy-Magnum; p.107 C. Lénars; p. 108 top Pratt-Pries-Diaf; bottom Berry-Magnum; p.109 Berry-Magnum; p.110 Pratt-Pries-Diaf; p.111 Pratt-Pries-Diaf; p.112 Berry-Magnum; p.113 top Blouin-Diaf; bottom Pratt-Pries-Diaf; p.114 left Barbey-Magnum; right Berry-Magnum; p.115 N. Singh; p.116 top Ledoux-Cedri; bottom Pratt-Pries-Diaf; p.117 Nardin-Explorer; p.118 Pratt-Pries-Diaf; p.119 Bajande-Rapho; p.120 top Pratt-Pries-Diaf; bottom Lapierre-Cedri; p.121 Girard-Rapho; p.122 left Pratt-Pries-Diaf; right Pratt-Pries-Diaf; p.123 Funk-Rapho; p.124 top Serraillier-Rapho; bottom Martin-Guillou-Explorer; p.125 Pratt-Pries-Diaf; p.126 Girard-Rapho; p.127 Girard-Rapho; p.128 top Pertuisot-Pix; bottom Degommier-Diaf; p.129 C. Lénars; p.130 Gérard-Explorer; p.131 Blouin-Diaf; p.132 Girard-

Rapho; p.133 top Mike Yamashita-Colorific!; bottom Régent-Diaf; p.134 Gérard-Explorer; p.135 Gérard-Explorer; p.136 top Gérard-Explorer; bottom Rowan-Ana; p.137 left Rowan-Ana; right Girard-Rapho; p.138 top The Image Bank; bottom Moulu-Vandystadt; p.139 Gérard-Explorer; p.140 top Moulu-Vandystadt; bottom Degommier-Diaf; p.141 Régent-Diaf; p.142 Budnik-Cosmos; p.143 M. Guillard-Scope; p.144 left Beuzen-Explorer; right M. Guillard-Scope; p.145 Dup-Explorer; p.146 Schoenahl-Diaf; p.147 Gould-Scope; p.148 top Pratt-Pries-Diaf; bottom Gould-Scope; p.149 Gould-Scope; p.150 M. Tulane; p.151 left Pratt-Pries-Diaf; right Pratt-Pries-Diaf; p.152 Lessing-Magnum; p.153 Pratt-Pries-Diaf; p.154 Pratt-Pries-Diaf; p.155 top Lessing-Magnum; bottom Gould-Scope; p.156 Pratt-Pries-Diaf; p.157 Tony Craddock-Tony Stone Worldwide; p.158 Vautier-de Nanxe; p.159 left S. Bellows; right Gould-Scope; p.160 top Pratt-Pries-Diaf; bottom S. Held; p.161 Pratt-Pries-Diaf; p.162 Fagot-Pix; p.163 Pratt-Pries-Diaf; p.164 top Pratt-Pries-Diaf; bottom Vautier-de Nanxe; p.165 Vautier-de Nanxe; p.166 Gould-Scope; p.167 du Authier-Diaf; p.168 top Garcin-Diaf; bottom N. Hochman; p.169 Garcin-Diaf; p.170 Kérébel-Diaf; p.171 top N. Hochman; bottom N. Hochman; p.172 Garcin-Diaf; p.173 Garcin-Diaf; p.174 Kim Hart; p.175 left The Image Bank; right Robert Francis-Robert Harding Picture Library; p.176 top M. Guillard-Scope; bottom E. Bataille; p.177 Garcin-Diaf; p.178 E. Bataille; p.179 C. Lénars; p.180 top Kérébel-Diaf; bottom Kérébel-Diaf; p.181 C. Lénars; p.182 Blouin-Diaf; p.183 left J. Privat; right C. Lénars; p.184 Schoenahl-Diaf; p.185 J. Privat; p.186 Schoenahl-Diaf.

Cover pictures:
Top: Andy Williams/Robert Harding Picture Library
Bottom: Picturepoint, London